Praise for *Letters to a Future*

This is more than "just" a golf book. It is a portrayal of the bond that existed between a student and her mentor; a relationship of understanding, hope, faith, and trust. It is a narrative of humility and generosity. It is a chronicle of aspiration, doubt, disappointment, reassurance, encouragement, and success. And it is an account of mutual admiration, respect, and friendship. All of these characteristics combine to form the human spirit, which is very much in evidence in these chapters.

— Ian Pattinson, Chairman - The Royal and Ancient Golf Club of St. Andrews, Scotland

I absolutely loved this heartwarming book. Dottie Pepper is an American original and revered for her decades of insightful coverage as a broadcasting giant. Now, she presents a must-read for anyone who loves the game of golf. We learn the encouragement and endless search for excellence it takes to be a champion.

— Norah O'Donnell, CBS Evening News Anchor and Managing Editor

This book easily could have been called *Letters from the Heart*. As with her illustrious golf career, Dottie has poured her all — and especially her heart — into this poignant memoir of the timeless lessons that Mr. Pulver gave her. Lessons that hold true today. Most important, she has shared with the reader her love of the game and of life. Read this book! It's a rare chance to see what gives a champion her toughness and compassion.

— Joe Hallett, 2018 PGA National Horton Smith Award, Golf Top 100, teammate of Dottie's at Furman University

I don't know too many people who work harder — at anything — than does Dottie Pepper. I also don't know too many people with a bigger heart. Now a window into where it all comes from opens in the beautifully told story of a remarkable man and Dottie and the relationship that helped forge it all. *Letters to a Future Champion* is one part diary, one part instruction manual, all wrapped up in a page-turning scrapbook come to life.

— Jimmy Roberts, NBC Sports

Passion has long been Dottie Pepper's co-pilot. Whether wielding an iron or holding a microphone, Dottie's been a glowing example of commitment to craft, dedication to good deeds, and loyalty to the deserved. Now Dottie wonderfully brings to life a magical three-ring binder of hundreds of letters and notes she shared with golf teacher George Pulver, Sr., who also kept an equal amount of correspondence from his pupil and friend. In this splendidly paced salute, Dottie rings up a timeline that champions friendship, honors the game and its traditions, and pays homage to an extremely kind man. This book comes from the heart. It will warm yours.

— Steve DiMeglio, Senior Golf Writer, USA Today/Golfweek

Dottie's sharing of Mr. Pulver's wise teachings about golf and life in *Letters to a Future Champion* allows Dottie and Mr. Pulver to give us the best of their collective wisdom. This book is a gift to cherish.

— Pam Shriver, International Tennis Hall of Famer, Olympic gold medalist, ESPN broadcaster

Golf being among the loneliest sports, Dottie Pepper gives us a beautiful reminder that no one does it alone. More than sharing the growth and development and success and setbacks of her game, she shares a selfless professional named George Pulver. Most remarkable about this book is how the voice and character of Mr. Pulver come to life in letters, most of which end with "no reply expected." It's all about giving.

— Doug Ferguson, Golf Writer, The Associated Press

McGregor Links, Saratoga Springs, New York

LETTERS TO A FUTURE CHAMPION

My Time with Mr. Pulver

By Dottie Pepper

MISSION POINT PRESS

Published by Mission Point Press
2554 Chandler Road
Traverse City, Michigan 49696

Hardcover ISBN: 978-1-954786-02-8
Softcover ISBN: 978-1-954786-29-5
Library of Congress Control Number: 2021901990
Second printing

Cover photography credits:

The photograph of George J. Pulver, Sr., in his workshop at
McGregor Links is courtesy of Jean Hague.
The photograph of Dottie Pepper with the trophy is courtesy of Jeff
Hornback. The back-cover photograph of Dottie putting is courtesy the
USGA Museum. (The trophy and putting photographs are not included
in the leather-bound edition.)

Printed in the United States of America
by Walsworth Publishing Co., Inc.,
Marceline, Missouri

Available for purchase at www.dottiepepper.net.
For bulk purchases, contact vlharrigan@bellsouth.net.

To
D.M.N.
who will not resent
the fact that he
is not mentioned
in this book

George J. Pulver, Sr., circa 1912

TABLE OF CONTENTS

Foreword by Kathy Whitworth

When Dottie asked me to write a foreword for her book, I was surprised and flattered. Surprised because we haven't been in touch for a while and certainly flattered as it isn't every day you are asked for a favor of such importance by such a great player and personality.

I began to notice Dottie shortly after she joined the tour in 1988. In fact, we played briefly together that year. (More on that below.) Where I really began to know Dottie, though, was in the inaugural 1990 Solheim Cup. I was fortunate enough to be named the U.S. team's captain. We had only eight players that first year, and Dottie was one of them. What I liked most about Dottie was her competitive spirit, her determination, and her even-keeled emotion.

The other players on the team included Betsy King, Beth Daniel, Pat Bradley, Patty Sheehan, Nancy Lopez, Rosie Jones, and Cathy Gerring. These players were the best in the world. Sure, the Europeans had some very good competitors. But we had the upper hand. Looking back now, I feel my best pairing was Dottie and Cathy. Both had the same attitude and very similar games. As it turned out, they played great. Not surprisingly, they became very close friends afterwards.

In Dottie's *Letters to a Champion: My Time with Mr. Pulver,* you will begin to understand who helped her become the champion and person she is today. Interestingly for me, it brings back memories of my own mentor and instructor, Harvey Penick. Best known now as the author of the *Little Red Book,* he was head professional at the Austin Country Club.

I was sent to see Harvey by the head professional of the Jal Country Club, Hardy Loudermilk. I was 17 and had been playing about two years, so I was fortunate to get to him at an early age. There is no question my success in golf was because of Harvey. He was perfect for me, although he said he wasn't right for everyone. When he first saw me hit balls on the range, he told me he thought he could help ... "but you have to do what I say," he said. Otherwise, it would be a waste of my time and his. Fortunately, I possessed enough good sense to say "okay."

He told me later that it's the student who makes the teacher, which I immediately disputed. Regardless, if I hadn't done what he'd asked, I would never have succeeded the way I did. Some of the things he taught me: a great grip, how to take "dead aim," how to shift my weight, and how to control the path of the club going back and the path coming down. He also taught me how to hit the grass in front of the ball going through, which keeps your head and eyes focused on what you're trying to hit and releases the club head at impact.

My very first lesson with Harvey was about the grip. I had just three days to work with him on it, so it became pretty intense. "The grip isn't the only thing, it's just the first thing," Harvey said. So, if I didn't get the grip down first, little else would matter. He told me to take the club back "like you were working by the hour, not by the job." Never having had a job, I wasn't quite sure what he meant — but I figured it out. Take the club back slowly.

Harvey also never focused on what you were doing wrong. He reasoned, "Why think about what's wrong? Just focus on what's right."

Harvey's influence was widespread. He also mentored Tom Kite , Ben Crenshaw, and Betsy Rawls. All three are in the World Golf Hall of Fame. He also coached the University of Texas team for many years, and almost all of his players became very accomplished.

So, I did play once with Dottie. It was in the opening two rounds of the Boston Five Classic in Danvers, Massachusetts. It was Dottie's rookie year. Dottie tells me that I chastised myself for hitting such a lousy putt at the last hole — #9. "Damn it, Whit," she heard me fume to myself. "They should just take your card." In fact, it went in the hole — and I made the cut. Obviously, I was focusing too much on what might go wrong. Harvey was right.

There are always people in our lives who have a significant impact on how we grow. I know this. Dottie knows this. Dottie is now sharing the time she shared with George Pulver, Sr. It is a compelling story of a quiet, loving man, a love of golf, and how those two forces combined to shape Dottie into the champion she became. From that history, there are lessons for all of us.

During her career, Kathy Whitworth won 88 LPGA Tour tournaments, a record number by a single golfer in both the LPGA and PGA. She is a member of the World Golf Hall of Fame.

Introduction by Dottie

For nearly forty years, I've had a now well-worn, three-ring binder. In that binder is every letter my beloved golf teacher, George J. Pulver, Sr., wrote me over the course of our time together. Letters came to me after every lesson and often more frequently than that. In the many times that I moved to a new location, the binder never once saw a moving truck. It was physically with me, because it *is* me and it *was* him.

Filled with years of his mostly typewritten letters, it was my reference book for all things golf. But as time has gone on, I've come to realize the binder is much more. It is a blueprint for honoring the history and traditions of the game of golf; it also is about mentorship, fundamental beliefs, curiosity, grit, grace, dreams, disappointment, success, and the value of education.

I had thought for some time that Mr. Pulver's letters would be a wonderful book. There was so much in them that needed to be shared, and shared not just with the golf world but with others in all sports, particularly youth sports. The letters transcend a teacher-student relationship. But who really has the time to leap into a book project of this magnitude? I had mentioned the idea to a few people, and they thought it was a good idea. But that's an easy response from friends. Getting it done? That's not so easy.

And then came March 2020.

With the Covid-19 lockdowns, I, like many others, suddenly had plenty of time on my hands and started cleaning out closets, boxes, file folders, and the like.

Among the file folders I emptied was one that contained many golf-instruction articles collected by Mr. Pulver. He called such articles "forbidden material," because he didn't want those instructions to conflict with what he was teaching me.

I figured that now, after 34 years, it was okay to break one of his rules, so I took a look. Not surprisingly, many of the articles contained his thoughts, whether pro or con, written in the margins.

What I did not expect to find in that ragged folder was every letter I had written to him, as well as letters my parents had written, thanking him for his work.

You may recall that paper products, including tissues, were in short supply in March and April of 2020. Fittingly, there were not enough tissues within reach as I dug through the folder, re-reading my letters and my parents' letters. This elusive project took on an entirely new and urgent dimension for me, as I began to understand just how much our relationship meant to him as well.

My original intent was to publish a book of just the letters, with short notes attached, letting the letters be the voice. However, three close advisers—let's just call them the "Three Wise Men" — convinced me to use Mr. Pulver's letters and our relationship as a mirror to my evolution in the game … to show how my abilities grew, how my beliefs about the game formed and shifted, and how I labored through the trappings of youth and college sports to emerge a professional who fully knows the grind it takes to be the best at anything.

This book was not an easy task, mainly because while I love talking about golf and sports — heck, I even get paid to talk about golf now—I do not like talking about myself.

The process was introspective and sometimes uncomfortable, even painful. It also forced me to formally put on paper the distillation of many of my own beliefs about character and competition after seeing both success and disaster among those I competed against or now observe from the sidelines.

Mr. Pulver's knowledge needs to be shared, because it is timeless and has so many applications, not just in sports but in education, business, and finding some balance in a world that sometimes seems to be spinning out of control.

My hope is that you have been blessed by a person in your life as special as Mr. Pulver was in mine. Or, if not, that person awaits you.

Or, maybe, you can be a Mr. Pulver for some youngster with his or her own big dreams and ambitions.

Thank you for reading.

— Dottie Pepper, April 2021

Dottie and Mr. Pulver, 1984, at Duffer's Den.

About the Funding of this Book

The money used to pay for this self-published project has its genesis in a Tuesday afternoon shoot-out at the 1993 LPGA Sun-Times Challenge. I won $5,000, which I deposited the next week into an annuity account. I left it untouched until this project became a reality. After 28 years, the cost of doing this book was almost exactly the pre-tax value of that fund. Some things are just meant to be.

A portion of the proceeds of the book will go directly to the programming efforts of the Saratoga WarHorse. The Saratoga WarHorse is a veteran-run 501(c)(3) serving military veterans and service members living with post-traumatic stress throughout the United States.

The organization's mission is to improve the physical, mental, and emotional health of veterans with post-traumatic stress by providing a healing, equine-assisted experience using off-the-track thoroughbreds.

There is absolutely no cost for veterans to participate, and the organization is 100 percent funded by charitable contributions.

For more information, go to www.saratogawarhorse.org.

LETTERS TO A FUTURE CHAMPION

My Time with Mr. Pulver

By Dottie Pepper

Chapter 1

March 4, 1980

My father, Don Pepper, Jr., left the game of baseball in 1971 after being one of the most promising players in the game. He signed with the Detroit Tigers the day he graduated from Saratoga High School in Upstate New York, working his way through the minor leagues and appearing on the cover of *Sports Illustrated* in March 1968 as one of baseball's hottest prospects.

Called up to the majors for what he terms "half a cup of coffee," he was ultimately traded in baseball's 1969 expansion to the Montreal Expos. But his father had passed in early 1967, leaving the family farm's operation to his mother and two younger brothers. Given the likely AAA Vancouver assignment with the Expos, he felt an obligation to return home to run the turkey farm, an operation of 45,000 turkeys raised and processed annually.

When the farm and many other similar farms were put out of business by expanded state and federal regulations in 1971, Dad turned to insurance and sales-rep businesses to provide for our family. Like so many other former baseball players, he also turned to golf for not only recreation but for competition. He also had a vision for now-unused farmland three miles north of Saratoga Springs.

On a portion of it, he built a 9-hole pitch and putt golf course and driving range, which was lit for night use; it also had a well-manicured practice green. I worked the counter, picked up golf balls from the range, cooked hot dogs, helped mow, and hit balls until my hands bled. I was hopelessly hooked — a raw talent that my dad had nurtured, helped along by reading golf magazines and him applying to golf what he knew from baseball.

And this is when and where my now 40-plus-year relationship with the Pulver family begins.

Don Pepper, Jr., second from right, poses with the town supervisor at a ribbon-cutting to open Duffer's Den. Dottie is at the far right; her sister Jackie is at the far left. Steve Worth, second from left, was Don's right-hand man.

When I first met George Pulver, Sr., he had long since retired from being an active PGA professional, but he was still very much involved in the game. By 1971, he had designed and completed construction of nearby Brookhaven Golf Club for the International Paper Corp. and remained involved in the club's agronomy. At age 9, I was a junior member there for $100 per season, playing most of my golf at Brookhaven with my paternal grandmother. She had introduced me to the game, bought my first set of clubs and given me a series of five lessons from a journeyman golf professional at Murphy's Driving Range in Saratoga Springs.

My first actual holes played were at the Par 29 course in the Saratoga Spa State Park, but my first "big course" golf was at Brookhaven.

We would often see Mr. Pulver and his wife, Martha, there on late afternoons. Impeccably dressed, he always wore a straw hat and usually a smart blazer as well. She also played and did so extremely well. Mrs. Pulver was a solid competitor in one of the local ladies leagues that I played in as a youngster. At Brookhaven he would walk along with her, taking soil samples, then offer a few thoughts about her swing. When I look back on them now, they so remind me of Carl and Ellie Fredricksen, the couple in the 2009 hit movie "Up." Although George and Martha had three children, unlike the childless Fredricksens, the love and admiration they had for each other was unmistakable. They were adorable.

They would make the drive to our driving range, Duffer's Den, on a fairly regular basis. I remember being at work and getting very excited to see their brown Toyota Camry pull into the parking lot. He was a local legend, and it was learning time! Mrs. Pulver would hit a

Above, George and Martha Pulver. Below, George with his dog, Fritz.

casual bucket; he would offer advice now and again. A few times, when she was visiting, their youngest daughter, Madelyn, would join them. Madelyn could really play! I would watch from afar, trying to soak up whatever I could. I cannot recall ever seeing him hit a shot, but he was constantly tinkering with his wife's clubs — a waggle here, a small strip of lead tape there.

By the late 1970s, my family had also become members at McGregor Links Country Club, then an inland Devereaux Emmett masterpiece, a very short bike ride from home and from Duffer's Den. It was a golf course that made me better in every way. Mr. Pulver had been at McGregor in some capacity — from caddy master to golf professional and greenskeeper to manager or the last three in combination from 1922 to 1962, having befriended the architect in the early 1920s.

I was champing at the bit to take my game to bigger competitions locally, in the state and beyond, struggling to find ways to know what tournaments existed and how to enter them. There simply weren't many competitive opportunities for junior girls in our area. Most of my competition came from either playing in local ladies events or against the junior boys in the area. By my early teens I knew I wanted to play golf in college and eventually on the biggest stage, the LPGA Tour. My big worry was gaining exposure to those college programs and coaches even though there were few tournaments for girls in Upstate New York.

Hence this letter of March 4:

March 4, 1980

Dear Mr. and Mrs. Pulver,

Hi! How have you been this winter? Great, I hope.

If it's not too much trouble I would like to ask a favor of you.

With the golf season coming up and many tournaments and dates being announced, I was wondering if you would keep your eye out for _any_ national or state tournaments and qualifiers.

I thought that you two would be the best people to ask to "watch out" seeing as though PGA magazines and things like that are addressed to you.

Dave Lewis at McGregor tends to throw entry blanks to tournaments out left and right and not tell me about anything. I've been trying to watch myself but it's not too easy when you get just the Schenectady Gazette and Golf Digest.

"Please watch for me and let me know if you hit 'gold.'" — Dottie Pepper

I read in the paper this morning where McGregor is having a tournament in Tom Creary's honor. I'm going to have to go to see the elder Mr. Dennis to see if I can play in it. I sure hope I can.

Well - thank you.
    Please watch for me and let me know if you hit "gold".

    Thanks again.
    Love,

    Dottie Pepper

P.S. Mrs. Pulver,
    If you are playing Intercounty again this year, I would love to play with you. I'd like to play with both you and Mr. Pulver sometime at Brookhaven.

    Dottie

One of George's golf clubs that I display in my home.

George J. Pulver, Sr., Timeline *1898-1947*

George Pulver Birth: March 23, 1898, in Saratoga Springs, New York.

Enters Albany Business College. Gains skill in shorthand and typing. First in family to attend college.

1920

Enlists in the U.S. Army and fights alongside the British Army for four years. Sees action in World War I in Belgium and France. Shot in leg, gassed in trenches. Rank: 2nd lieutenant.

1916-1920

1909

Begins caddying at the Saratoga Golf Club. Earns 15 cents per round. Each lost ball costs him 15 cents. He also works after caddying at the polo fields near the golf course as a groom.

Becomes both a scholar and athlete at Saratoga Springs High School. Later, the McGregor Links Foundation will provide the annual George J. Pulver Scholar-Athlete Award to an outstanding Saratoga Springs High School female and male graduate.

1922

A cub reporter at the *Saratogian,* is directed by the paper's owner, Capt. Jack Walbridge, to "take this new book by Seymour Dunn, read it and report it to me. You are the only one I know who understands golf language." Dunn wrote using Scottish derivation, making it difficult to understand. George's job is to make it readable. Develops friendship with Dunn. Begins work at McGregor Links as caddy master.

Becomes professional, manager, and greenskeeper at McGregor Links. He would serve in this capacity until March 20, 1962.

On August 3, marries Martha Walsh. George met Martha at the British Colonial Resort in Nassau where they both were employed for the winter season. Martha's sister was also working for the hotel. The Walsh sisters were from Providence, Rhode Island.

1924

Sets the then-course record of 70 at McGregor Links on Sept. 8.

1925

Appointed club manager at McGregor Links. Retains title until 1961.

1927-1961

Wins the Northeastern New York Open Golf Championship at Albany Country Club. A 6-shot victory over the reigning national PGA champion, Tom Creavy, and the highlight of his playing career. "Joy that night on the 17th hole at McGregor Links," Pulver writes. The Pulvers live right of the 17th fairway.

1932

Madelyn Jennings remembers her father walking home early evenings over the 17th hole singing, "Don't Fence Me In." Both sisters – Madelyn and Jean Hague – never remember their father acting stressed, regardless of the number of children or number of clubs he managed.

1929-1941 Winter-season golf pro at Tarpon Springs, Florida.

1936

Nine-hole course at Saratoga Spa opens. George becomes first manager. Will give up position at end of 1936 season. For a short time, manages all three Saratoga golf courses.

1926-1927

Serves as golf professional in Nassau during winter seasons.

1933-1972

Golf Professional Saratoga Golf and Polo Club (formerly Saratoga Golf Club) and architect of a newly conceived nine-hole course at the Saratoga Spa.

Qualifies for the PGA Championship at Blue Mound Country Club, Milwaukee, Wisconsin.

1923

Becomes Dunn's assistant at the Lake Placid Club golf course. Both spend winters teaching golf in New York City on the third floor of the A.G. Spaulding sporting goods store.

Shoots a course-record 66 on Nassau. Score is confirmed by Devereaux Emmett, who designed McGregor Links. Dunn and Emmett were Scottish colleagues; Dunn gets Emmett to give Pulver job in Bahamas.

George J. Pulver, Sr., Timeline

1948-1995

Works full-time at McGregor Links in December 1941, when Pearl Harbor is attacked. That day, the family leaves Saratoga for New York for the night. As they enter the city, paper boys wave the news: "Pearl Harbor Bombed!" They hear FDR declare war. They continue to Tarpon Springs for the winter season.

1941

"Golf almost did not exist during the war," recalls Jean Hague. Adds Madelyn Jennings: "Some of the war years, my mother and father did defense work for GE (General Electric) in Schenectady."

Construction work begins on first nine holes at Brookhaven G.C. These 9 holes would open for play in August 1963. Project was done as a health and recreation benefit for the employees of the International Paper Corporation.

1961

Final nine holes open at Brookhaven G.C.

1971

1950-1980
Consults as golf-course architect or agronomist on Sacandaga G.C., Nick Stoner G.C., Antlers C.C., Bend Of The River G.C., Top Of The World Golf Resort, Queensbury C.C., and Glens Falls C.C.

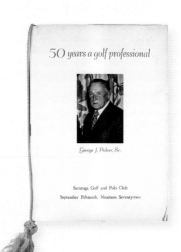

50 years a golf professional

George J. Pulver, Sr.

Saratoga Golf and Polo Club
September Fifteenth, Nineteen Seventy-two

1972
Testimonial dinner is held Sept. 15 for George, observing his 50th anniversary as a golf professional.

Dies Thursday, Jan. 16, at 87 years old at his residence after battling a long illness.

Dottie Pepper was in her junior year at Furman University. George was still coaching Dottie at age 87.

1986

1981
Wife, Martha Walsh Pulver, dies on March 13.

Dottie Pepper begins working with George in April. She had played just a bit of golf with Martha at Brookhaven prior to working with George.

1995
George is inducted into the Northeastern New York PGA Hall of Fame. Pulver was a 60-year member of the PGA and a founder of the Northeastern New York PGA.

"He always called it a matchless, undiminished determination and the will to win. He always told me it's not the wins and losses but rather the manner in which you search for excellence that remains to the very end." — Dottie Pepper

I had the privilege of taking one lesson from the referenced Tom Creavy somewhere around 1977 or 1978. I knew he was the 1931 PGA Champion but had no idea that Mr. Pulver had beaten him to win a significant championship in our area while Creavy was still reigning national champion. Mr. Pulver hated talking about himself. Absolutely hated it!

My ending note to Mrs. Pulver shows how eager I was to learn from the best in a competitive setting. She was a former club champion, and the Pulvers were considered golfing royalty locally. Her unexpected but personal response arrived soon after I wrote seeking help. Even in her final years she was a graceful player, a quiet and respected entrant in local ladies' league competitions.

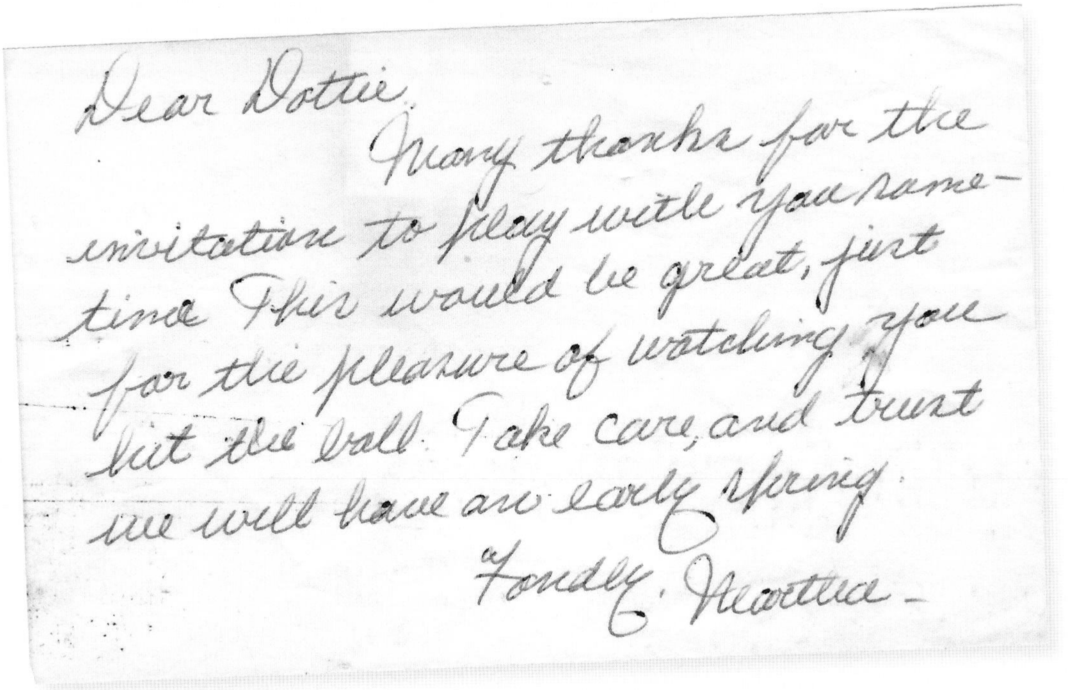

Dear Dottie,

Many thanks for the invitation to play with you some-time. This would be great, just for the pleasure of watching you hit the ball. Take care, and trust we will have an early spring.

Fondly, Martha —

This painting of Martha Pulver hangs in the pro shop of McGregor Links with a similar painting of George Pulver. (See George's portrait on Page 187.) Photo courtesy of McGregor Links.

Mrs. Pulver's note here was a follow-up to my initial "Help, please" letter and rediscovered in my Tupperware "tidbit" box that I took to college. How it got there, I have no idea, but I found it in April 2020 while looking for a picture hanger. I needed that hanger for a piece that was given to me by the town of Greenfield, New York, for my work with their junior golf camps.

The photo's subject: the long view across the 18th green at Brookhaven to the foothills of the Adirondacks. It's a small world.

Mr. Pulver preferred to correspond using his typewriter, a comfortable link to his days as a cub reporter for the *Saratogian*.

At right is the first formal letter I received from Mr. and Mrs. Pulver. Note the first sentence of the fifth paragraph. "Do not be discouraged." That theme will present itself throughout the letters to come. I was discouraged because getting tournament information was difficult, and I often found that my young age limited my access to some better events.

Some of those restrictions, as he predicted, did ease as my skills improved and it became apparent that I could compete with the best in our area. Perhaps most important was that the owner of McGregor Links allowed me to play in the morning tee times with better players on the weekends, rather than being restricted to afternoon times set aside for juniors and beginners.

"Certain restrictions have been built up through many years in golf tournaments, which may seem at (times) obnoxious, and frustrating. You may later agree that they have a place." — *George Pulver*

March 15, 1980

Dottie:

It was nice to get your note. I shall scan my mail as it comes to hand, and will certainly forward to you any golf material which may pertain to your interest.

At this point in time, I do not have access to a profusion of golf data, but I am still a member of The P. G. A., and the Greens Supt., of America, hence do receive some mailings.

Bert Edwards, probably gets the important club mail. He is in Florida at the present time but as soon as he returns, I shall mail him a copy of this letter. I am certain he will gladly gather pertinent golf activities. As you may know, Brookhaven, is a member of both the U. S. G. A. and the New York Sate associations, and should receive all notices.

I am less than certain how the Creavy Tournament contestants will be accepted. However, since Creavy spent his major teaching hours with women players, I would assume a Memorial Tournament to his name would include a women's division. It could be hoped, that provisions for Juniors would be included in such a tournament.

Do not be discouraged. Certain restrictions have been built up through many years in golf tournaments, which may seem at time obnoxious, and frustrating. You may later agree that they have a place. However, down the road, your skill and your charm, will open many doors to you.

Good luck, and best wishes to your mother, father, and grandmother. Martha shares these felicitations.

Miss Dottie Pepper
Worth Road,
Gansevoort, N. Y. 12866

Geo & M Pulver

P. S. I enclose a recent U. S. G. A. formx that is characteristic of all such forms from State or National Golf Bodies. Such forms contain information that contestants should scrutinize. No reply is expected.

This letter, dated Aug. 2, 1980, arrived after I lost in the final of the NYS Girls Junior Championship to Oak Hill's (Rochester) Jamie DeWeese. Jamie was the heavy favorite in the match and a top national college recruit, but as a 14-year-old, I gave her a good run.

A year earlier I had made my debut in the Girls Junior, losing to Winged Foot's Pamela Darmstadt after tying for medalist honors in stroke play qualifying. Losses to girls who played their golf at big name clubs were helping me develop a bit of a "Little Engine That Could" attitude, but it was also helping me develop a chip on my shoulder and an "I'll show you" mentality. As a family we moved out of our house each horse racing season in Saratoga, the rent money allowing me to play golf tournaments. It was a bit of "have vs. have not" for me.

Dottie at the 1979 NYS Girls Junior Championship, her first. She would lose in the quarterfinals.

"The one huge difficulty you must overcome will be to learn to putt and play to hard, fast greens." — *George Pulver*

August 2, 1980
136 East Ave.,
Saratoga Springs, N. Y. 12866

DOTTIE:

Martha and I congratulate you on your recent effort in the State
Junior Tournament. For one to finish second in any endeavor even
in a small town is noteworthy. To finish second within your county
is a feat, but to finish second in your state, this must be a staggering
accomplishment.

One perhaps learns more from defeats, that perhaps from victories. "A
very fine line exists between the thrill of victory, and the agony of
defeat."

You are very young--proceed slowly. I have always felt that fine
mechanics and power to be enormous aids to success in sports. Yet
there always comes a time, when something more intangible will be
needed. Concentration--The will to win--Never give up, these must
be the mental qualities that distinguishes the champions from the
runner-ups. Certainly no one would pick Trevino, to be one of the
greatest golfers of the past decade.

The one huge difficulty you must overcome will be to learn to putt
and play to fast, hard greens. Few such courses exists in this area.
Burdensome costs, rules out, all but a very few courses, from providing
championship challenges.

The girl you lost to, in the Junior finals, came off those lightning
greens of Oak Hill. She has been competing since Pee Wee tournaments,
no doubt encouraged by zealous well-healed parents. Oak Hill can afford
championship conditions. Initiation Fees, $5000, Dues, $1000 a year--
I know.

Do not get discouraged--you will find a way. Pick your spots. Every
tournament you play in will add to your confidence and skill.

Please no reply. Suffice you should know you carry our good wishes,
and interest. Say hello, to your Father and Mother.

                    Sincerely,
                    George, & Martha Pulver.

Miss Dottie Pepper,
Worth Road,
Gansvoort, N. Y.

The letter was a template for many future letters: perspective, encouragement, examples of tour players I could relate to. Mr. Pulver was always positive in tone but also realistic in sharing what he knew my challenges would be.

We did not have a teacher-student relationship yet, but Mr. Pulver began molding in me the qualities that all champions have — a head and heart built to win.

The 1980 PGA Junior Championship in Palm Beach Gardens, Florida, when I was 15 years old was my first national competition. The national PGA paid for one girl and one boy from each of its 41 sections to make the weeklong trip. It would prove an important event on my calendar for three consecutive summers and one that eventually helped pave my way to a golf scholarship at Furman University.

Another common theme shows up early: Don't be in any big hurry. Mr. Pulver must have sensed that I was looking at the things I did NOT accomplish through the summer and yet wanting to move at an even faster pace. Note his positive tone yet again. His final comment is still one of my favorites today.

As an avid reader and one whose appetite for learning was never satisfied, Mr. Pulver always had an arsenal of great quotes. They certainly came in handy with a certain youngster who wasn't blessed with a lot of patience and who had big growing pains.

"The course is fantastic – it has fast-hard greens. I'm adjusting to them." — Dottie Pepper

Copy Please!

August 28, 1980
136 East Ave.,
Saratoga Springs, N. Y. 12866

DOTTIE!

YOU, have done wonderful with your golf this year.

YOU, were low qualifier, State of New York, P. G. A.
Juniors
YOU, went to Florida, and facing the best in the country
accomplished much, under new and strange conditions.

YOU, returned and was second in the huge Gazette tournament,
beating distinguished district players, many of whom were
four years older, and had a vast amount of Winter College
Golf competition under their belts.

YOUR, efforts exceeded the most sanguine expectations.

We join your many friends in congratulations, in your
recent golf success.

Miss Dottie Pepper,   Sincerely,
Worth Road,
Gansvoort, N. Y.

                    George & Martha Pulver.
                    *George
                    & Martha*

 P. S. Well done--keep at it, but proceed slowly. The old
German proverb comes to mind: "Those who run too fast, often
stumble."

"YOUR, efforts exceeded the most sanguine expectations." — George Pulver

12-15-80

Dear Mr. and Mrs. Pulver,

I can't thank the two of you enough for everything you have done for me the past year. I will forever cherish and follow your advice. Your beautiful letters have really helped me get over the "rough spots" and "growing pains" this past spring and summer. I still get those "growing pains" when I see the juniors that travel a lot and win all of the major junior championships. But I always return to your letters again and again for the strength to get me through. I realize that that their horizons will all be met before I am through dreaming about mine. I am going to take it slowly and let my game and myself mature at the rate that it wants to - not at the rate that the local golf critics want it to. You have given me the best advice I'll ever get.

This past summer has been one that I will always remember. I would have never gotten through the pressure filled moments if I didn't have your wisdom-filled letters to turn to. One line in particular will always stay in the back

-2-

of my mind: "Proceed slowly. The old German proverb says, "Those who run too fast, often stumble." I think I will walk, instead of run!!!

I wish you both the happiest and the best of all Holiday Seasons.

Love to both of you,
Dottie Pepper

A Christmas thank you. I had already begun a collection of Mr. and Mrs. Pulver's letters, a resource I would reference throughout my entire playing career (and beyond) as I saw their applicability not just to today's junior and amateur golf worlds but all youth and amateur sports.

Winter and ski season had arrived, but these letters would be the guidance and foundation for planning my 1981 schedule and the upcoming months of indoor practice.

"I always return to your letters again and again for the energy to get me through." — Dottie Pepper

Golf didn't stop for me in the winter. Dad built me a very rudimentary chipping area in our basement from an old bed sheet hung from the beams and a small piece of AstroTurf. I also spent hours putting on the kitchen and family room carpets as the balls rolled a speedy 10 on the stimpmeter — a device used to measure the speed of a putting green — and even had a bit of break in spots.

It was during these winter months that I would make a big decision about golf. I would also see an enormous change in my relationship with Mr. Pulver.

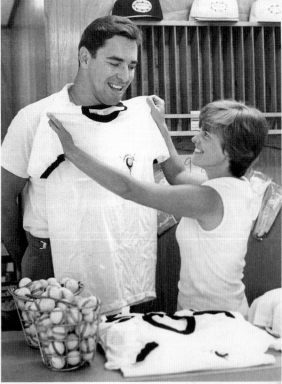

Above, Dottie and her dad in the early days of Duffer's Den.
At right, Dottie's mom and dad on opening day at Duffer's Den.

TOURNAMENT RECORD

1978 (Age 12-13)

- Runner-up, Brookhaven C.C. Ladies Club Championship

- Winner, Brookhaven C.C. Cuna Cup Championship

- Winner, Hansel and Gretel Championship, McGregor Links C.C.

1979 (Age 13-14)

- Winner, Northeastern Junior Girls Championship

- Lost in quarterfinals, New York State Junior Girls Championship

- Winner, Brookhaven C.C. Ladies Club Championship

- Winner, Hansel and Gretel Championship, McGregor Links C.C.

1980 (Age 14-15)

- Winner, PGA National Junior Section Qualifier (Northeastern New York)

- Lost in finals, New York State Junior Girls Championship

- 30th place, PGA National Junior Championship

- Second place, Gazette Women's Amateur Championship

- Winner, Brookhaven C.C. Ladies Club Championship

- Winner, Schenectady Golf Association Falling Leaves Championship

Chapter 2

Sports, not just golf, played a huge role in my upbringing. My maternal grandparents owned the Alpine Sport Shop in Saratoga Springs, New York — in fact, the shop is still in the family, and 2020 marked its 80th year in business. I skied from the time I could walk and, if pressed to choose a favorite today, I would probably still grab my boards and head for the mountains. I, of course, had grandiose dreams of racing, dreams that were quickly extinguished by my parents because of cost, time, and the poor odds that one would actually succeed, let alone have a reliable income as an adult.

Dad was an exceptional skier and became a gifted instructor after baseball. I turned my winter attention in that direction, becoming a junior ski school instructor at Gore Mountain, just an hour north of home, when I was 15. I was busy: I worked in the ski shop on a fairly regular basis. I studied hard at school as a mostly straight-A student, and I worked in the ski school program every weekend.

Every other free moment, though, I was pitching and putting at home. Golf certainly was not my singular focus, but I still loved it.

It helped that Mr. Pulver continued to write to me over the winter. He shared what I believe to be one of his most important letters in late January 1981, referring to a response he had in September 1980 to an excellent column written by Lou Torre at the Gazette.

In the column, Lou made these key points:

• Long hours can and will interfere with family life and holidays.

• There is often a lack of job security.

• You must be prepared to wear many hats and be your own public relations person.

• This career choice will shape your entire life, both positively and negatively.

Lou's column is still a relevant and realistic assessment of the rigors and challenges of not only being a club professional but, as Mr. Pulver said in his letter to me, for "young people with their eyes in the stars, marching toward a career on the tour."

The NYS Women's Amateur Championship trophy presentation with Betty Deeley.

January 27, 1980
136 East Ave.,
Saratoga Springs, N. Y. 12866

DOTTIE:

Your note of Dec. 15th, I deem a unusual one, from a very unusual person.
Let me first assert, in which Martha joins, you are entirely too extravagant
in your praise of our tiny help.

In my view at avery early age, you are comprehending many salient and
undying fundamental facts about the strivings around you .

Golf is a game of a lifetime. Out in the fields under God's blue sky, it
is a game which challenges not only ones control and skill, but immense
and formidable mental and psycological processes as well. But it is only
a game. Clearly look to your preceptions and good common sense to guide
you.

Finally -- Listen to your Father and Mother. Avoid gut courses at school,
such as sociolgy or psycology, unless you choose such as a field. Always
try to have something solid to hold on to, until you can grasp something
better, down the road.

I meet young people with their eyes in the stars, marching toward a career
on the tour. I have said to them:"Unless you can defeat everyone within
three hundred miles of your home, four out of five times, pause and review
your thinking and your goals."

All the seasonal well wishes to your father and mother, and your aunt,
and your good self.

George & Martha Pulver.

P. S. I feel that Lou Torre, to be the most knowledgeable golf scribe
in the Capital district during the past 30 years. Recently, I responded
to one of his golf readers. His story and a copy of my response attached.
There may be a slight chance some of this material may catch your interest.
I hasten to point out, however, that my attitudes and conclusions must be
held in suspect, because of my years. With this in mind, you are meminded
to screen carefully my remarks.

PLEASE RETURN ARTICLE AND MY COPY AT YOUR CONVENIENCE.

*"Unless you can defeat everyone within three hundred miles of your home, four out of five times,
pause and review your thinking and your goals."* — George Pulver

Jackie (Pepper) Diehl

Growing up as a younger sibling to a gifted, driven athlete can be pretty tough — tough to sacrifice your own summer vacations to travel to the others' competitions, tough to form your own identity.

My sister was always her own person, and I owe her enormous thanks for also being shoulder to shoulder with me through some pretty wonderful times in my career. She never loved the game as I did; she definitely preferred skiing and wasn't a huge fan of hot weather in general.

But she, too, absorbed Mr. Pulver's instruction like a sponge, and I would put her up against anyone reading greens. She successfully caddied for me in my first U.S. Women's Open qualifier (1984) and the championship itself, and got me through the 1987 LPGA qualifying school despite my case of the shanks.

Jackie and Dottie at the 1985 Colonie Open Championship.

One of our finest and funniest learning experiences came at the U.S. Women's Open qualifier in 1987. With no yardage books available, we walked and charted what we thought was the qualifying course before the event. Little did we know we walked one of the wrong nines at the 27-hole facility.

It ultimately didn't matter much as I ended up being medalist at the qualifier and tied for 12th in the championship itself.

In late February the entire junior ski school was skiing out of bounds, as youth will do, cutting from one portion of the mountain to another on an access road. What could possibly go wrong in a full tuck on a rugged, un-groomed access road? Three hairline fractures later — and a glove that had to be cut off because of the swelling in my left wrist — I had the answer: four to six weeks in a cast.

The math was pretty clear. Even if things went well, the start of my golf season was likely now in jeopardy. I was back on the mountain the next weekend with a huge mitten over the cast, but I knew that an early start to the golf season was out. It got even worse when my mother discovered that I was continuing to hit pitch shots with the cast on. Needless to say, the two-week check-in with the doc coupled with her intel meant that the four-week option was no longer on the table. Because of those pitch shots, the doctor extended my recovery to the full six weeks.

If losing the ability to do something you love makes you appreciate it even more, I got a big dose of that. Realizing I might compromise my golf season or have some sort of complication in rehab made me double down on golf. I still would teach at Gore in the junior program the next winter, but my high-speed antics were over.

I did not spill the beans about my spill in a letter to Mr. Pulver's daughter, Madelyn. But at the time, with a more focused approach to golf, I knew I needed help. First, I wanted to offer my best to Madelyn, given Mrs. Pulver's illness. Second, I thought it'd be better to approach Madelyn rather than Mr. Pulver directly to see if he would take me on as a student. I knew he could fill that void better than anyone.

What I didn't realize then was that Mrs. Pulver was failing rapidly. Yet four days before her death, and despite all that was happening at home, Mr. Pulver committed to helping me. To put such thought into a letter (see Page 27) at a time like that still makes me marvel at his strength.

We would be filling voids for each other at just the perfect time.

Dottie Pepper
Box 191 Worth Road
Gansevoort, New York 12831
February 27, 1981

Dear Madelyn,

Thank you very much for keeping me posted on both your mother and father's conditions. It came as quite a shock to me. I knew that she was not well but I never dream it would be this serious. My sympathy goes out to you all. If there is anything that I can do, please let me know. My phone number is 587-0506. Please let me help with anything.

This spring I will be in need of a golf coach. I thought that I would ask you first, if your father would be interested at all. I don't want to interfere with him spending time with your mother or any other plans he may have. I have been thinking about this for a long time. If he doesn't want to — I understand completely. I think so much of him and his knowledge and experience with the game. I know he would be the best! He is such a fantastic person.

My game needs fine tuning and I need a mental game with confidence now. I just think he would be the absolute best - anywhere. I wouldn't need much of his time at all. Please ask him for me when the time and place seems appropriate. Other pros that I have gone to want me to be their student to be able to "put a feather in their cap." I know your

A tradition would soon begin when after each lesson, within a day or two, a summary letter would be left in my family's mailbox. The letters were simple, direct, and always based on the fundamentals. I still believe this to be the very best way to teach and learn golf — or anything for that matter. When players ask me to take a look at a part of their game or they share what they've been working on, I usually ask if they have been writing down their own observations — what seems to work, what seems to not work.

It's how I learned from Mr. Pulver, but it's also a great way to become more self-sufficient when things inevitably get a bit off the tracks. Mr. Pulver did that writing for me, but it was and is still easily referenced.

— 3 —

Dottie Pepper
Box 191 Worth Road
Gansevoort, New York 12831

dad wouldn't do that and he wouldn't push me into big tournament until he and I both knew I was ready.

Well — I will close for now. Thank you. Best wishes to all of you.

Love,
Dottie

March 9, 1981
136 East Ave.,
Saratoga Springs, N. Y. 12866

Dottie:

Madelyn passed your letter along to me, as well as her comments.
She scores you as high on maturity and intellect, as I do your
Golf. Thanks for the nice things you said about me. Your aim is
far above the target, but thanks anyway.

Now as to your golf, and my tiny help. My plans and routines are
in dismay, but I will get back to you later, down the road. One
day, I would like to look at your swing at greater length, rather than
the heretofore fleeting glance.

A good golf style is indeed desirable, yet there is more. Your swing
has served you well -- do not attempt radical changes. Time will
support changes as needed. Cosmetic changes perhaps, with the years,
but everyone must find his or her own way of attacking a golf ball.

I have witnessed the bent left arm of Varden. The majestic sway
and lurch of Hagen. Trevino, who appears to be beating an annimal
on his down swing. Lopez with her sudden starting away wrist cock.
Yet these Titans of golf past and present had more:

        THEY HAD REPEATING SWINGS.
        THE WILL TO WIN.
        ENORMOUS CONCENTRATION, UNDER A THOUSAND EYES.
        AND FINALLY--THE MOST IMPORTANT SHOT IN GOLF**
        THE ONE BEING PLAYED.

Keep working on your putting. The oldtimers putted with bent elbows,
and wristy hand action. The new order, employ extended arms, and
firm wrists. In my view, stiffer competition and rewards--faster
greens, to say nothing of architectural machinations, have forced
acceptance of this surer method.

Please do not bother to reply. Should I have any thoughts, I will
send them to you. At this point, it seems to me that you are preparing
your golf schedule with wisdom. No compensation is implied. Publicity
holds no charm for me, and I sort of cling to the background.

Please say hello, to your father and mother.

Miss Dottie Pepper,   George J. Pulver, Sr.
Box 191 Worth Road,
Gansevoort, N. Y.

"The oldtimers putted with bent elbows, and wristy hand action. The new order employ extended arms, and firm wrists. In my view, stiffer competition and rewards — faster greens, to say nothing of architectural machinations, have forced acceptance of this surer method." — George Pulver

April 25, 1981
136 East Ave.,
Saratoga Springs, N. Y.

DOTTIE:

It was a pleasure to watch you hit a few golf balls. If from time
to time, I feel constrained to write you, its because my mind is old,
and slow, and my initial responses are often inadequate. Recap:

    1. Square up your foot and shoulder line in your power
clubs, These lines should roughtly follow the target line.

    2. START BACK SLOW AND LOW.

    3. THE MOST IMPORTANT SHOT IS THE ONE BEING PLAYED'.

    4. Play in as many nearby tournaments as convenient.
Nothing will take the place of experience on different
courses and grasses.

    4. When playing becomes boring, rest until you find yourself
eager to get back on the golf course.

    5. Remember, what I recommend to you is not etched in stone,
it can be changed. No once should make major changes in your
swing -- it is better than good.

    Sincerely,

Miss Dottie Pepper,
    Worth Road,
      Wilton, N. Y.

P. S. It was nice to see your mother --she looks well. Say
hello, to your father.   NO REPLY --I look forward to seeing
you in two weeks.

I was finally out of the cast, with no complications from the breaks, when in late May, I managed to slam my left thumb in a car door while getting ready to play a women's amateur event in Albany. Another three weeks on the sidelines! Now, being ready to play in the upcoming Women's State Amateur was really looking dicey.

Leave it to Mr. Pulver to use this time to pivot my learning in a different and very valuable direction.

Mr. Pulver not only left me summary letters, he left me books to read. He loved to read, loved to write, and loved to explore everything about the game, its characters, and its places. And I was a sponge for every drop of knowledge he was willing to share.

His first book assignment was Sam Snead's *The Education of a Golfer*. Released in 1962, the paperback cost 50 cents. To me, it has been worth millions, not just in dollars but in understanding the unquestionable ability of the greats to find a way to get the most of themselves, to evaluate their opponents, and to find sanity in a game that can so easily drive you mad.

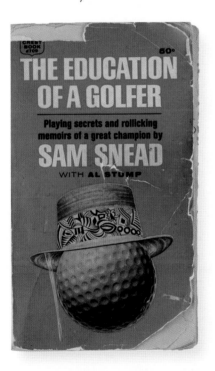

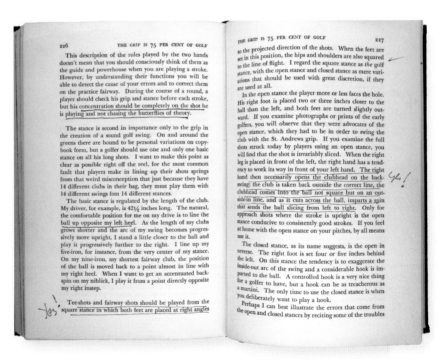

Mr. Pulver had underlined passages throughout the well-used book — basic mechanics, tempo, golfing temperament, rules, putting — everything he thought important was marked. I absorbed the stories of Snead's humble roots, huge wins, playing for money he didn't really have to lose, brutal losses — all of it.

"What I recommend to you is not etched in stone, it can be changed. No one should make major changes in your swing — it is better than good." — *George Pulver*

June 10, 1981

DOTTIE:

Please read this early book by Snead. Of course, much is fictional, and anecdotal in this book, yet between the lines will be found jewels of competitive wisdom.

You have better than a good swing -- it has advanced you well early. Of course, all swings can profitably be finer tuned. But top golf is more than this. It is the mental and tempermental factors -- the desire to win -- the sweat and tears -- the denunciations -- these are the things which produce a great athlete.

Here we have in Snead, a player certainly no intellectual giant. Yet, from excruciating and painful competitive experiences, he has extracted the very essense of championship golf.

Study his words. Sponge up what appeals to your reason, reject that which personally makes no sense to you, but somewhere in that little book lies golf.

Snead is really an athletic phenomenon. He plodded his way, to one of the great golf records of all golf history. But much more -- in spite of his limited education and peasant surroundings, he brought to his game, one of the most penetrating golf intellects of almost any player in my lifetime.

In all human endeaver, there always comes a time when inherant wisdom equates and often exceeds scholarly wisdom. Snead clearly had the former. Repetitive swings will come with time, and the beating of many balls, but it is never too early to arrive at a golf philosophy. I trust this this little book may help.

George J.

Miss Dottie Pepper:

"Snead plodded his way, to one of the great golf records of all golf history. But much more — in spite of his limited education and peasant surroundings, he brought to his game, one of the most penetrating golf intellects of almost any player in my lifetime." — George Pulver

Sam Snead at the 1952 Masters.
Photo courtesy of Augusta National Golf Club.

I read and re-read that book waiting for my thumb to heal, and it became my go-to all summer, so much so that I did a page outline of the highlights, knowing I would need to return Mr. Pulver's original. You can imagine my great joy when, after Mr. Pulver's death, his family gave me a significant portion of his golf library, including this book.

Today, I send this book to others on occasion and only ask that they read it, soak up what they like, discard what they don't, and then — as Mr. Pulver would have said — "Please return at your convenience."

On June 24, I sent a belated Father's Day note to Mr. Pulver.

Aside from the miss on grammar — "solider" — the letter acknowledged the importance of what I had learned so far from his teaching. What were those things?

June 24, 1981

To a very special person that has helped me tremendously this season. You have helped me create a much solider golf swing plus the desire and will to win.

I apologize for being so late but I hope you had a great Father's Day.

Love,
Dottie

Three, mainly:

1. Fine-tuning the speed of long putts

2. Finding my own way and touch, whether it be with my right hand or left

3. Changing my ball flight from a weak fade to a powerful, chasing draw.

The last would become my preferred shot shape; it was how my eye saw golf courses for the rest of my playing career. I had a cut that, as my good friend Kandi Comer says, "only hooked a little." But that draw was the go-to. I did what Mr. Pulver recommended in leaving the fades to "special shots or to the muscle people."

Mr. Pulver would not accept any money for his help, so Mom would often bake for him or I would use my savings from work at the ski shop to buy him sweaters. I learned he would never postpone a lesson because of lousy weather. He would wear his dress hat, add layers under a sport coat, and occasionally sport a pair of corduroys on the coldest of days. It set the example for being ready to play in any conditions.

The next eight weeks changed the direction of my junior and amateur career. It also changed my belief in myself. I not only became the youngest player to win the New York State Women's Amateur but quickly followed that by winning the New York State Girls Junior, the only player to ever win both in the same season.

Photo by AP Laserphoto

'oung Champion

ifteen-year-old Dottie Pepper of Saratoga Saturday captured e New York State Golf Association Women's Amateur Championship at Rome Country Club. Pepper defeated Joan Placek of Northport, 4-3 in the last match. At left, Pepper is driving off the 15th tee. At right, she's jubilant after sinking her winning putt on the same hole.

Dottie kept newspaper clippings of her tournament successes, this one from the Post-Star *capturing her win at the NYS Golf Association Women's Amateur Championship in 1981.*

The Women's Amateur win seemed to pretty much come from nowhere. I'd never entered that championship and had been injured twice in the months leading up to it. But the basics Mr. Pulver and I had worked on in conjunction with the gems from the Snead book were pure gold. He kept the lessons simple, stressing time-tested fundamentals but also emphasizing how much heart and will it would take to win anywhere. I had not played much match play, but the Snead book came up big there, too. Snead wrote of knowing he "had" an opponent when that opponent changed his pre-shot routine under pressure. I saw it happen in one of my matches, and sure enough, I had her.

There were many lessons learned in that win at Rome Country Club, including how to play when spectators were openly rooting against you and managing the anxiety of a complicated ruling involving advice and an outside agency. (The issue was so complicated, it necessitated a call to the USGA in Far Hills, New Jersey.) Dad's baseball experience definitely helped me get through the first issue. But all of this was much more manageable thanks to the simplicity of Mr. Pulver's teaching and his wise choice of reading material for his student.

After my win, on July 15 my mother wrote a letter to Mr. Pulver describing my transformation. "She has absorbed your teaching like dry ground absorbs rain," she wrote. That was so true … like a sponge.

Dottie is playing a completely different game of golf than a year ago. Sure, she can hit the ball further, but the girl I watched for 5 difficult matches played a mental game I thought she was not capable of at such an early age. Her attitude and confidence went unshakable under severe pressure by older, more experienced players. Even Kathy Lawrence from Canton, who played a rude, unsportsman like game from the first hole on Friday, could not rattle her. Kathy's gallery even clapped and cheered at a couple of Dottie's missed shots. Dottie completely ignored it all and attacked her game like a tiger. Her concentration was intense. Mr. Pulver, this is attributed to you. So many times I asked her how she handled a situation during her game and she always quoted what you have been telling her all spring. She has absorbed your teaching like dry ground absorbs the rain.

July 19, 1981
136 East Ave.,
Saratoga Springs, N. Y. 12866

Dear Mrs. Pepper:

Generally, I feel comfortable with the written word. Your
gracious letter of July 15, however, causes me to wonder if
I can adequately respond.

Of course, Dottie is playing better. She is a year older, and
more experienced. Her match with Kathy Lawrence exposed her to
the mental and tempermental factors of golf. Such factors are
faced by champions in every sport.

Dottie should continue to seek competition -- but pick her spots.
Only in such a wayshall concentration and the urge to win be
developed. At times, even the Gods may seem arrayed against her.
Still, she must continue to push herself to do her best -- though
every muscle cries out to quit.

Yet, Golf is but a game. Lets not filch from her, the precious moments
of her youth. When golf ceases to give her pleasure, she should cast
aside her clubs until playing and competition again beckons.

Thanks for everything, and above all lets welcome her the same,
when she loses as when she wins. The losses today provide the
experince to goin the wins of tomorrow.

Mrs. Donald Pepper,   Sincerely,
Box 191 Worth Road,
Gansevoort, N. Y. 12831   George J. Pulver.

P. S. Constantly, I am observing her mechanics. Should she stray from
her usual excellent application, I shall persuade her to get back into
hergroove.

Mr. Pulver promptly wrote back, cautioning to not let others "filch from her, the precious moments of her youth."

At the time, there was quite the buzz around our area and beyond about my Women's Amateur win. But Mr. Pulver's steadying advice in the wake of victory is so apparent in the letter.

Teen better than par for the course

Pepper practices swing

Greg Luckenbaugh photo

By GREG LUCKENBAUGH
Sports Writer

Finely-tuned visions of the future usually do not reside in the minds of teenage girls. Immediate concerns, like skin complexion or getting a date with the cute boy in english class, usually dominate.

But for 15-year-old Dottie Pepper, a Wilton resident who recently won the New York State Women's Amateur Golf Tournament, the future does not amount to worrying what clothes to wear tomorrow.

"I guess I am different from a lot of my friends," said Pepper, whose age and looks belie her golf talents. "They don't have the slightest idea of what they want to do."

Pepper knows precisely what she wants to do — be a professional golfer.

Being a professional athlete, while a dream of many, is attained by few. In her case, however, that goal may not be so elusive.

"I think she's the most exciting women's golfer I've seen in this area in 60 years," said 83-year-old George Pulver, who has coached Pepper for the past year and was a golf pro at McGregor Links for 40 years. "She has a keen and serious mind. When the pressure's on, a keen mind has more avenues to turn to than the dumb clucker who just blasts the ball and uses his animal instincts."

"All the great champions have had the keen mind — Hogan, Jones, all of them," he continued. "I don't want to build her up too much, but she's an unusual girl."

Pulver's high praise of Pepper is hardly unfounded.

In winning New York's most prestigious golfing event for women amateurs, Pepper went head-to-head in match competition with seven veteran golfers, of which the youngest was 21. Two years ago, she lost in the quarterfinals to the eventual winner, but shot a sizzling 72 in defeat.

She also finished second at the New York State Junior Championships last summer, in competition with the best 18-year-old-and-under female golfers in the state.

In addition, she has won a host of lesser tournaments in the area.

In spite of her youth, Pepper has the dedication of a time-hardened veteran.

She plays no sports other than golf at Saratoga High School, not only because she'd rather concentrate solely on golf, but because she says they interfere with her studies. She maintains a 95 average in school.

"The coaches have asked me to try out for the other sports, but I don't want to risk the injuries," she said.

The only other sport she participates in is downhill skiing, and even that gave her grief.

"I broke my wrist doing that last winter, and I spent the whole winter worrying about how it would effect my golf game," she said, in spite of the injury.

Pepper still teaches skiing at Gore Mountain to keep active during the off-season.

Her mother, Lynn, believes this off-season is a blessing in disguise.

"A lot of people tell us we should send her south for the winter so she can play golf year-round," Lynn said, "but by the time October rolls around, she's ready to burn the clubs. The break is good for her."

Pepper, who has been playing competitively for just four seasons, won the junior division of the first tournament she ever played in when she was 11. She lost the overall title in sudden death, however, to the woman who first taught her to play, her grandmother.

"She got me going in golf when I was 8. When I started golfing seriously at 11, my father became my coach," Pepper recalled. "It's been my father who has taught me most of what I know."

According to Pulver, Pepper's father did an excellent tutoring job.

"I'm a teacher who believes that if it works, don't fix it," Pulver said. "When I first saw her swing, I could see she did very little wrong. I'm working on the psychological part of her game, rather than her mechanics."

Pepper says she has come a long way in that aspect.

"In the past, I used to crack under pressure, or be bothered when I heard other players mumbling 'she doesn't belong here,' because I was so young," she said.

But Pepper did not fold under the pressure of the amateur championship, although she probably had good reason to.

"They (the older players) gave her the business," Pulver said. "When you've been golfing for a while, and suddenly you've got a 15-year-old hitting the ball better than you, you'll use every bit of gamesmanship you can use. They did, but she stayed with it."

It is difficult being both talented and young in a sport that has rarely seen talented teenagers, but Pepper will not be so out of place when she golfs Sunday in the qualifying round of the New York State Junior Championship at Oswego.

After that, the next biggie is the National PGA Junior Championship at West Palm Beach, Fla., on Aug. 18. Last summer, Pepper played poorly and finished 25th out of 50. This year, she hopes to finish in the top 10.

As for her not-so-immediate future, there are plans of first playing college golf in the south (she has already sent inquiry letters to several colleges), and then turning pro.

"We can never know what makes a champion," Pulver said, pondering the possibility of Pepper being a pro. "A lot of cold days and a lot of hot suns are necessary before we can know.

At 45, Pepper should have more than her share of such suns and days to prove herself.

A newspaper clipping from the Post-Star, spotted with Dottie's glue marks, profiles her early tournament success.

I wish I could include portions of this letter in every youth sports' introductory information: about choosing your competitive spots and his advice that youngsters need to push themselves when everything is stacked against them, but also to understand how important a life is away from competitive sports. Let it be their choice to push harder, not their parents'. Let wins and losses be welcomed the same, especially in golf when we lose so much more than we win.

Also important at this time was the way Mr. Pulver got back to work with me without giving the Women's Amateur win excessive attention — it was a long journey and we simply had a great start.

Starting the backswing slowly was always a big thing with him, something I look for in players now, or even when I hit a few balls myself. This was a simple idea, easy to lean on, and flawless in the "cauldron of competition," as he referred to it.

I felt enormous pressure leading up to the Girls Junior tournament, not only because I was chasing a two-tournament win — something that had never been done before — but because of my own expectations after losing in the final the previous summer.

I wrote this letter to Mr. Pulver ahead of the event, assuring him that I now felt ready to face the pressure.

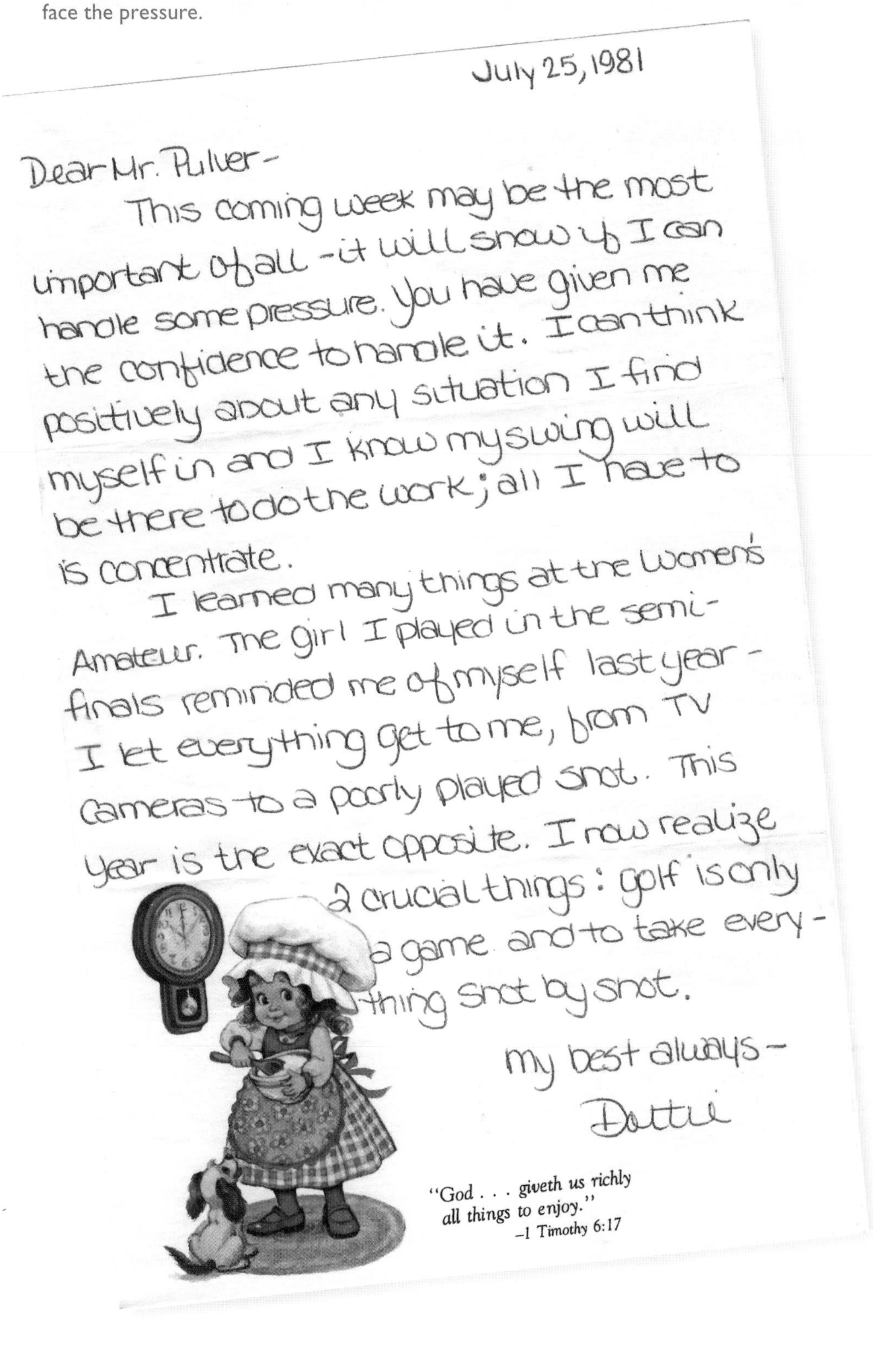

July 25, 1981

Dear Mr. Pulver —

This coming week may be the most important of all — it will show if I can handle some pressure. You have given me the confidence to handle it. I can think positively about any situation I find myself in and I know my swing will be there to do the work; all I have to is concentrate.

I learned many things at the Women's Amateur. The girl I played in the semi-finals reminded me of myself last year — I let everything get to me, from TV cameras to a poorly played shot. This year is the exact opposite. I now realize 2 crucial things: golf is only a game. and to take every-thing shot by shot.

my best always —

Dottie

"God . . . giveth us richly all things to enjoy."
—1 Timothy 6:17

Like it was for the Women's Amateur, my grandparents' motor home was headquarters for tournament week. There was no money for a hotel. We ate in every night, mostly from food brought from my grandfather's garden. I had one pair of good golf shoes that were stuffed with newspaper and "baked" in the oven to dry after a cold, rainy day in the middle of the week. I wore the same $10 powder blue Kmart shorts that I wore in my win at Rome Country Club.

I took pride in being scrappy, gritty. I went on to beat a player from Oak Hill in the semis, Diane Nixon. But it was important to push on, to finish this off in "Little Engine That Could" style. And I did. I beat Kathy Hart in the final. It was a big deal, because she was such a good player and her dad was a PGA professional. She even dressed like a professional golfer.

The win was met with great joy at home, not only from the Pulver family but also the club members at McGregor Links who threw a big party for me. Madelyn gave me a beautiful silver necklace engraved with the dates of the two championship match wins. It is still a piece I wear today. I'm so appreciative of how the entire Pulver family supported the relationship their dad and I had.

Dottie accepts the trophy from Betty Deeley at the 1981 NYS Junior Girls Championship. At left, the runner-up, Kathy Hart.

Despite the victory, I remember being sad and pretty torn at the party. I had to be all in on the adults' celebration, greet everyone and, of course, give a few comments on the big wins. But I really wanted to just be with my friends, goofing off in the pool. I eventually gathered up enough courage to ask for permission to do just that. In hindsight, I'm glad I did. Too often in junior golf and other youth sports, kids are not allowed to be kids. Instead, adults live their lives through them, robbing the kids of innocent, childhood fun.

Very quickly, I returned to practice and playing. Mr. Pulver, in turn, continued his helpful instruction in this letter of Aug. 7. He was adding layers to my understanding of the golf swing, this time focusing on the beginning of the downswing.

August 7, 1981

DOTTIE:

The last time I wrote you, I said the most important key in starting back to be -- Start back slowly, keeping club face square to ball.

Now I add another key: Start the downswing by shifting your left hip straight at the target.

Bobby Jones says: "The first motion in starting the downswing must originate in the hip"

Ben Hogan writes: To start down forget everything else and turn your left hip to the left.

The great Snead and the heroic Palmer counsel -- Pull the club down on the inside with the left hand and arm.

Toski, Pate, et all, allege they start down by moving the left knee to the left to start down.

Take your pick, but there remains one thing certain, weight shifting preceeds the twisting of the hips to the rear. This will promote power, and insure a more inside blow, and aid in getting the ball air-born in spite of a tight lie.

Spend time and focus on the regular trap shot. Variations can be learned later. I think your swing for this shot to be excellent-- you may have to use slightly less wrists at the top. REMEMBER -- watch the spot of ground you wish to hit, not the back of the ball as you would in other shots.

If possible, do not play winter rules. Play the ball as it lies even near the greens. In no other way, shall you learn to play tight lies, without trepidation. This is one of the reasons, the last session we had, I encouraged you to move the ball back slight- ly, and shift your weight, that the club head would approach the ball and meet it, just before the low part of the arc. This not only get the ball air bound, but spins the ball which one needs to alight on fast greens.

George,

P. S. Tell Jackie, to loosen her shoulders and her knees -- the club only weight about a pound and the ball but a scant 1 3/4's of an ounce. Sneak those hands a little more on top of the club, even if the ball flies to the right some.

He consistently added players for reference throughout our time together, urging me to find a player or players I could best relate to.

I also so admired him for looking out for my sister, Jackie. Four and a half years younger, she often tagged along when I went for a lesson. He encouraged her as well. She must have been listening well because she often caddied for me through amateur golf, got me through the LPGA qualifying school despite my case of the shanks, and even caddied for me as a professional when her school schedule allowed.

The middle part of August wasn't nearly as fun as the start, with a loss at the biggest women's event in the area, the Gazette Women's Amateur. But Mr. Pulver never looked at losses as a negative, rather as an experience from which to learn and gain perspective. Sometimes it's much easier to say that than to do it, but he was always trying to find a way to get better, not just for me as a player-student but for him as a teacher.

One of my favorite things he ever wrote was on Aug. 25, in the second paragraph. He had such an ability to address pressure and mechanics — things we can control and things we cannot but always with a healthy eye toward the future.

August 25, 1981
136 East Ave.,
Saratoga Springs   N. Y. 12866.

DOTTIE:

Welcome back! You have done wonderfully well. To be sixth in the vast United States is super.

Pause and recollect! If it was pressure, it shall take time. If it is mechanics, we can do something about it. Should it be strange surroundings, and geography, experience is needed. Remember, from our defeats must one learn to succeed later down the road.

Pressure will always be present at important moments in your golf. Time and experience shall soften this pressure, but never entirely remove it.

The other day, on the screen, I witnessed one of the superior pressure players of our time, Hale Irwin, almost give away a tournament already in his hands. Three bogeys in a row, nearing the end of 72 holes, and the pressure showed in his agitation and dismay. Then in one supreme pressure packed moments, he holed a ten foot putt. Pressure appeared in this veteran of many championships notwithstanding.

Anytime you would like to resume our work, please advise. Bring Jackie along for a few minutes.

I STILL THINK YOU WERE GREAT!

MISS DOTTIE PEPPER,   George Pulver,
Box 191,
Worth Road,   Geo
Gansevoort, N. Y. 12831

"Remember, from our defeats must one learn to succeed later down the road." — George Pulver

Mr. Pulver loved Bobby Jones, and toward the end of the summer, Jones' book *Golf is my Game* arrived in the mailbox. Again, the book was marked with more underlining by Mr. Pulver. In this letter, he summarized the Jones mindset in one page. It was excellent guidance in how to manage mistakes and expectations, how to manage the golf course, and how to be flexible when you just don't have your best stuff — because that is most of the time.

Photo courtesy of Augusta National Golf Club

The next day, Mr. Pulver wrote a second letter, and this one could not have been more different. He switched from the psychological outlook of Bobby Jones to a bit of equipment education and then bunker play. His plan to turn out a well-rounded student of the game was becoming very apparent.

September 5, 1981

DOTTIE:

THIS IS A QUOTE BY BOBBY JONES --

"I was amazed to find that in some rounds, fairly good from
a scoring standpoint, I could find only one or two shots which
which had not been mishit to some degree. Many, of course, had
finished on the green or near the hole, but most had been hit a little
too high or too low on the club; some had faded or drawn when the
action had not been intended; some drives of good length had barely
missed the sweet spot.

I finally arrived at a sort of measure of expectancy that in a
season's play I could perform at my best rate for not more than
a half-dozen rounds, and that in any one of these rounds, I would
strike more than six shots other than putts, exactly as intended.
If one should have confidence in such an appraisal, which I had, the
following conclusions were inexcapable:

1. I must be prepared for the making of mistakes.

2. I must try always to select the shot to be played and
    the manner of playing it so as to provide the widest possible
    margin of error.

3. I must expect to have to do some scrambling and not be
    discouraged if the amount of it happens to be more than
    usual.

GJP

Golf Is My Game
p.166: Bobby Jones:

There is a school of Oriental philosophy, I am told, which
holds that the aim of life should be the perfection of
personality or character and that sufferings, joys, and
achievements mean nothing except as they influence
the development of this personality or character.

September 6, 1981

DOTTIE:

Always, and I repeat always, the heart of the golf club must be the
shaft. To get distance with a golf club one must produce speed. If
speed is produced, one must have stiffness for control, but as we
get stiffness, we get weight. The strong person can swing a stiff
shaft and heavy, without sacrificing loss of speed. The weaker player, however, requires the same stiffness to get requisite speed, yet
he cannot manage weight.

Hence, during the past ten years an effort has been made, led by the
Hogan Company, to produce a stiff but light shaft. Aluminum came
first -- it was light and strong but lacked feel. Graphite followed --
it was stiff and light, but tortion (club head wobble) developed, at
loss of control. Next light weight steel which provided stiffness,
lightness, and no club head twist. This is where we are today.

Your set of clubs is equipped with larger diameter, stiffer shafts.
I have added head weight to restore feel. We are seeking not greater
distance, but better timing of the club head. Try these four clubs for
a week or so and then make a judgement.

Keep practicing the basic trap shot. The short flop out from good
sandy lies -- 15 to 20 feet. Also think of the hardest sand shot of
all -- the longer shot from a good bunker lie -- perhaps 15 to 20
yards. Less sand, of course would be taken.

Go down into that trap on No. 1, and hit toward the club house.
Select the shallow part of the bunker, then try with your Wedge,
#8 iron, and even your #5 and 7 irons, and observe the distance produced.
For long shots out of good lies in a bunker, a rather full swing should
be used, the swing slow and smooth, and above all first anchor your feet
in the sand. These are really precision shots. A smidgeon of too little
or too much sand and the shot is ruined.

HANG IN THERE!

                    George,

The bunker referenced is the cross bunker at McGregor Links' opening hole. The variety of shots required to play the course, no doubt, was an asset to my development. But to have someone who had been around that course for such a significant portion of his professional life was an added advantage for me, since the course was less than a mile from home.

Having won two state championships during the summer and then finishing sixth in the PGA Junior, I felt an enormous amount of pressure to win the women's club championship at McGregor that fall. Mr. Pulver left no stone unturned in laying out a plan for success, including getting to the course unhurried and attacking from the first hole. End result: a 1-up win over Lois D'astalto.

"Win the first hole"

Joanne Gunderson Carner, aka "The Great Gundy" or "Big Momma," is a national treasure, a lovable character with a raspy laugh who also got great joy in winning and winning big.

She won 43 times on the LPGA tour, is a member of the LPGA and World Golf Hall of Fames, and one of the grittiest competitors I've ever known or had the privilege to learn from.

Photo courtesy of LPGA archives.

As I note in this chapter, it's because of her that I learned to excel at match play. Here's the story:

The U.S. team had lost the 1992 Solheim Cup at Dalmahoy, Scotland, and Joanne was chosen to lead the American team in avenging the upset loss. The matches were tied 5-5 after two days heading into the ten Sunday singles matches. As we gathered around the large table in the team room after Saturday's dinner, Joanne was asked for her advice going into a tension-filled final day. Her response: "Just go win the first hole."

I remember the anxiety vaporizing in the room as each team member now had a clear duty and focus, an aggressive mindset. The result was an 8-2 U.S. session win and a 13-7 overall victory.

It's a lesson of determination I've not forgotten.

As I went through my career, I came to love and appreciate match play, the momentum changes, and the prospect of playing someone head-on. Joanne Carner, my 1994 U.S. Solheim Cup captain, proved to be a big inspiration in getting me to embrace match play — partly because she was so darn good at it, winning a U.S. Girls Junior and five U.S. Women's Amateurs. But it was also because of her simple advice delivered with a cigarette in one hand and an adult beverage in the other:

"Just go win the first hole."

Photo courtesy of LPGA archives.

Mr. Pulver was similarly succinct, so when he spoke, you listened full in. Most of his letters were the same. He didn't write to fill space, he wrote to add greater, deeper knowledge, understanding, and self-belief. In this letter, he discussed pace, timing, and centrifugal force, and he exposed me to the notion of "a canard" in golf. That he could wrap all of this advice — plus references to five great players — in a tight letter took talent and thought.

October 11, 1981

DOTTIE:

As I observed you hit balls on Saturday, I could find little fault with your excellent swing. What mechanical errors seen, were the result of your timing. You were starting back and down too fast -- you were reaching your higher swing speeds too early. THIS IS WHAT I WOULD SUGGEST:

Everytime you practice hit a few casual #5 irons. Then pick-up your power clubs and try to capture the same pace. The power will come from the longer shaft and arc, and not from additional effort.

Players differ in pace, because of temperment and reflex-time. But there is one thing certain -- the long smooth swings of Jones, Snead, Littler, Nelson, and Caponi have added longevity to their talent.

Ponder on the word PACE, and TIMING. Also view the word Centrifugal Force as found in the dictionary.

And please understand, everyone is more or less nervous before and during a critical match. To allege they are not is a canard. However experience and time shall erase much of such misapprehension.

MISS DOTTIE PEPPER.

George,

"There is one thing certain — the long smooth swings of Jones, Snead, Littler, Nelson, and Caponi have added longevity to their talent." — George Pulver

He also sent along articles written by some of the greats, including Herbert Warren Wind. Forty-plus years later, daughter Madelyn still clips articles and sends them to me via mail — not email — just as her dad did.

With fall's arrival, I had time to consider my journey the previous summer. There were lots of highs and some lows. I felt I owed Mr. Pulver my own assessment of my progress. If I had any doubts rising from my difficult summer and then winter that I could succeed at golf, they seemed now to be gone.

October 29, 1981

Dear Mr. Pulver,

Thanks so much for passing this literature onto me. It made for some very interesting reading and it gave me an insight to what it takes to become a great champion such as Nicklaus, Watson, Hagen, Sarazen, Jones, and Hogan.

Lately I have had a chance to stop and think about my summer. You have helped me so much. Ever since that first cold, windy day in April, my mind and game have matured incredibly. I could not have done all that I did without you. I have become a more consistent player with 100 percent more confidence than I had last year at this time. Each time the pressure was really on me, I would stop and think of the basic fundamentals of the physical and, most of all, the mental game that you taught me. I have read and re-read all of the letters you have sent to the point that I have most of them memorized. I think that perhaps the one phrase I fall back on most

2.

often is, "Golf is only a game." Before each tournament or match I read those letters and they set me in the right frame of mind to attack the course and my competitors, to always do my best and to never give up. They have gotten me out of more than one bind. Many times I would get myself into a situation where I was not sure of what to do and I would ask myself, "Dottie, what would Mr. Pulver tell you what to do?" It would work every time- I would always hear you tell me the logical thing to do and I would do it and it always worked. The most helpful thing you told me about the swing is to start back low, slow and slightly inside. By keeping those three things in mind I hit a very risky shot in the semi-finals of the Womens Amateur. I hit a high, long draw over big trees to an elevated green to win the match. By relying on those three basics, my swing has matured by feel and it has become much solider. I can make a pass at the ball with a good amount of confidence.

3.

You have taught me more in the past year than I dreamed possible. My summer was more than I ever dreamed about. Your wisdom and knowledge has made me realize my love for the game and how great this game really is- win or lose. I have also realized that in golf, like anything else, I will only get as much out of i as I can put in.

Thanks so much for everything you have done and I hope this coming year is even better!

Love always-
Dottie

I received a thank-you note from Mr. Pulver on Nov. 2. It was short and modest: "I fear my efforts fail to match your words," he wrote. Yet, there was a telling line at the end that now rings so true.

November 2, 1981

Dottie:

After you left, I found your gracious note inside the Program.
I am extremely grateful for your kind words. I fear my tiny efforts
fail to match your words.

If in my remarks and notes to you, I seem to overstress the mental
and tempermental factors in this maddest of games, it is because
your swing was already better than good when I first looked at it.
You were ready to advance to the immense hurdles of golf -- the mental
ones.

Keep on matching. Detours shall arrive, but be not deterred. You have
already come a long way. Whatever your plans, get as much experience as
you can from amateur contests. Should you care to go beyond -- you will
be prepared for the cauldron.

Thanks for everything!

George,

Say hello to your father and mother, please.

"Keep on matching," he wrote. "Detours shall arrive, but be not deterred." He added: "Whatever your plans, get as much experience as you can from amateur contests. Should you care to go beyond — you will be prepared for the cauldron."

With winter upon us, I returned to my work at the ski shop and at Gore Mountain. During the weekends, though, I would often finish at the mountain around 4 p.m. and be home by 5, able to spend an hour to sit with Mr. Pulver in his living room and watch the end of golf telecasts. Talk about an opportunity to be a sponge. He would view and discuss the competition through his filters. I hope today's young golfers seek out the same opportunities with their mentors.

His final letter to me that year was a wonderful summation of the years' lessons. He referenced "a golf gem seed" being planted. I felt that I had enough for a full garden and then some! This particular letter is essentially a one-page stand-alone for everything he believed about teachers, students, competition, and complete preparation.

"Teachers of golf spend their lives and their energies sorting-out theories. Great players play by feel, not by theories. Do not get too cerebral. When you are faced with a shot, elect to play it in the simplest manner possible, and always play the shot you feel you can bring off."
— *George Pulver*

Dec. 20, 1981

DOTTIE:

It was nice to see you and your Father the other evening, and I enjoyed talking with both of you. That sweater is just wonderful, for size, style, and color. Two things about the sweater that I must remember -- DON'T put it on and keep it one until Spring, and prevent the covetous eyes of my son to see it, else it may take a Spring trip to Aspen.

GOLF POTPOURRI:

Always, as I talk to you, I am trying to expose you to different golf viewpoints. By all means reject those which makes little sense personally. It is my hope, that somewhere along the line a golf gem seed may be planted.

Teachers of golf spend their lives and their energies sorting-out theories. Great players play by feel, not by theories. Do not get too cerebral. When you are faced with a shot, elect to play it in the simplest manner possible and always play the shot you feel you can bring off. Relate to your own golf experience in the past as a guide. In the cauldron of competition, think only of the shot before you. God! alone how difficult this to be.

Need I remind you that you will have good days and bad days. The important thing, you must learn to score reasonably well on those days that you are not hitting pure shots. Scrambling whatever, I feel that champions in all sports reach deep inside of them, and continue to fight.

Tommy Armour, one of the golf giants, when asked if he was a great teacher, responded "Great players make the Great teachers great, and not the other way around."

Finally "The decisive factor between players of first rank, will be found to be the ability of certain players to continue to perform under the strain which all must feel." R. T. Jones.

It was nice to see your father and please say hello to both your father and mother.

MISS DOTTIE PEPPER,   George,
Worth Road,
Box 191
Gansevoort, N. Y. 12831.

By this time, after such a season, there was pressure by some, including my paternal grandmother, to consider not going to college and instead to turn pro right after high school. I was not aware of the conversation my mother apparently had with Mr. Pulver about this, but I never gave that possibility serious thought. I needed other options should my dreams not pan out — the open doors that a college degree could provide. It was a backup plan that Dad didn't have.

Mr. Pulver's opinion about my future was revealed more fully to me in a letter that he wrote to my mother.

"It seems to me a steady test through college golf might be the way to go — then to make a judgment," he wrote.

He added: "Moreover, should one jump right into tour efforts from high school, it is most likely they will be journeymen for a number of years, under terrific expense."

Mr. Pulver was indeed a very cautious, prepared man who liked to examine all sides of an issue, then present the facts so that a good decision could be made. He certainly had input on what would be an important decision about where I would get that degree and play college golf.

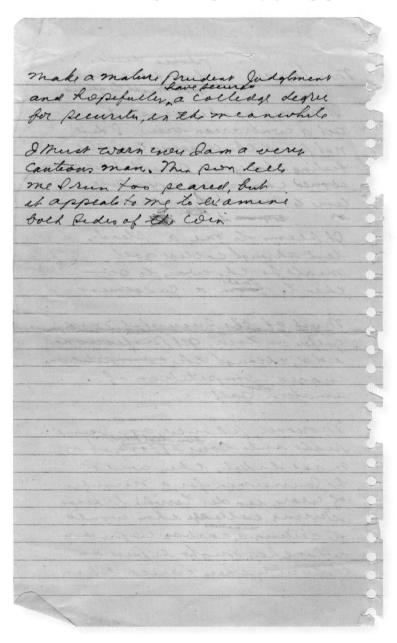

Dottie's grandparents' Winnebago – the campsite for the NYS Junior Girls Championship.

"You have better than a good swing — it has advanced you well early. Of course, all swings can profitably be finer tuned. But top golf is more than this. It is the mental and tempermental factors — the desire to win — the sweat and tears — the denunciations — these are the things which produce a great athlete." — George Pulver

TOURNAMENT RECORD

1981 (Age 15-16)

- Winner, Northeastern Golf Association Championship, McGregor Links C.C.

- Winner, New York State Women's Amateur Championship. (Youngest winner ever)

- Winner, PGA National Junior Section Qualifier (Northeastern New York)

- 6th place, Northeastern Pro-Junior Championship

- Winner, New York State Junior Girls Championship. (First player in state history to win both state titles in same year)

- 6th place, PGA National Junior Championship, PGA National Golf Club Palm Beach Gardens, FL

- 2nd place, Gazette Women's Amateur Championship

- Winner, Brookhaven C.C. Women's Club Championship

- Winner, McGregor Links C.C. Women's Club Championship

- 4th place, Boys Suburban Council Golf Championship

- 9th place, Boys Class A Section II Golf Championship

- 8th place, Boys Intersectionals, Willows C.C.

Chapter 3

Two wins in the New York state championships and a top 10 in the PGA Junior put me on the college recruiting map. Eighteen months earlier, I was very concerned that that was even a possibility. It was now time to start honing a college plan, a huge deal because I would be the first in my family to go to a four-year school. I also put enormous pressure on myself to prove that 1981 was no fluke for a small-town kid from Upstate New York. I continued to be a part of the junior ski school at Gore Mountain during the winter, but golf was my clear focus, unlike a year earlier.

Mr. Pulver constantly emphasized the value of higher education and was so pleased when I asked him to write a letter of recommendation that I could include in my college applications.

I sit in between Cheryl Morley, left, and Heather Farr after I finish second this year in the PGA National Junior Championship at Palm Beach Gardens, albeit a distant 10 shots behind Heather, unquestionably the best female junior player in the country. Photo courtesy of PGA of America

"Her mechanics are excellent. Her grip orthodox, her turn big, and the use of her lower body modern in every way. ... She is strong!" — George Pulver

March 1, 1982
136 East Ave.,
Saratoga Springs, N. Y. 12866

TO WHOM IT MAY CONCERN:

First let me say, I have been a class member of the P. G. A.,
since 1932, and I am still a member. I have worked many years
in Florida, several years at the Lake Placid Club, here in N. Y.
and for 40 years as head pro at McGregor Links, in Saratoga Springs.

Dorothy Pepper, I first saw bumping out balls several years ago,
at a nearby driving range. This past summer, I started to work seriously
on her game. Indeed, I liked what I saw!

Her mechanics are excellent. Her grip orthodox, her turn big, and
the use of her lower body modern in every way. At the top her club
points at the target, and her swing plane coincides with her height.
She is strong!

But enough of this sweetness. Desirable as a sound swing must be,
top level golf demands much more. The will to win -- The concentration
on the shot which is being played, and to keep fighting to the final
putt. I feel that Dorothy possesses these qualities.

Finally, and importantly. Dorothy has a keen intellect, she is an excellent student, and her philosophy mature. She has been a credit to
our area, and I feel she shall be a credit to any school which she may
attend. In my view, playing against her peers, to be the single ingredient most needed to advance her talent.

Yours truly,

George J. Pulver, P. G. A . card #M454876

With a background in the newspaper business, Mr. Pulver often communicated with the local golf writers, both with praise and criticism or correction. One of the greatest bits of advice I've been given as an announcer is to never let a mistake go uncorrected (thank you, Mike McQuade of ESPN).

Clearly, Mr. Pulver lived by that philosophy as well. In correcting a local scribe about the mistake in an article, he turned it into a teachable moment, giving further depth not only to the writer's knowledge but mine as well. History and architecture were a really big deal to Mr. Pulver.

April 1, 1982
136 East Ave.,
Saratoga Springs, N. Y. 12866

Dear Dick:

I write this note to correct the spelling of the name of the architect, who designed McGreger Links. His name was Devereaux Emmett. At the conclusion of World War I, it might be said the three most prominent golf architects in America to be Donald Ross, Stanley Thompson, a Devereaux Emmett.

I knew Devereaux Emmett very well! he not only designed McGreger here in Saratoga, but nearby Schuylers Meadows in Albany, St. George's on Long Island, a course in Bermuda, and several courses in Nassau, British West Indies.

He was most proud of being a direct decendent, of the Irish patriot Robert Emmett. He who was charged with creating an Irish rebellion. However, in spite of his magnificent extemperaneous speech in his own defense, he was hanged by the British, circa 1778-82.

Your mention of the New York State Amateur returning te McGreger in July. The first big tournament that I can recall being played at McGreger, was the 1926 New York State Amateur -- I was there. The tournament was won by a big strong boy, by the name of All Brodbeck, playing out of Siwaney.

Please consider this note to be a personal one, and no reply expected.

With every good wish, I am

Yours truly,

George J. Pulver, Sr.,

Mr. Dick Sirianna,
c/o Saratogian,
Lake Ave., City.

Mr. Pulver's handwritten notes, not just the typewritten ones, were also packed with wisdom, a bit of humor (describing the range balls used by the new owners of Duffer's Den as "turnips"), things to check off in preparation for tournaments (for example, a good umbrella), diet, playing with what you brought to the tournament instead of making major changes in competitive situations, and a huge one for him: learning to play by feel. I loved these notes because they seemed to be working documents, musings as his mind moved through the game and through my game.

April 25, 1982

Dottie:

It was a pleasure to see you hit some pure shots! Your Swing
looks better than last year -- more compact with no distance loss.
It might be a good idea if you applied that bandaid to your thumb
before you start hitting balls, not after.

If I were asked what areas of the swing most likely to break down
under pressure and fatigue, I would at once assert, starting down
from the top.

One may go back in many ways, but must approach the ball from the
INSIDE, coming down. This is the most important thing which I have
learned after sixty years of golf.

The culprit, of course, is the strong right hand and shoulder turning
too early in the start down. Many, including Snead, Armour, and the
ancient Scots, advised pulling down with the heel of the left hand,
and still others, Hogan, and Nicholaus, starting the downswing by
driving with the lower body. Find which works the best for you, and
practice and practice it. Should we not come to the ball from the
inside, we shall lose power, and perhaps go-over-the-top of the ball.
I don't want you to become too cerebral about the golf swing, but I
would be remiss, not to indicate pitfalls.

Please thank your mother for these squares. She cooks as well as you
golf.

No reply. We can discuss at the range.

George

Geo

His constructive humor and healthy chiding would continue to pop up throughout his letters, like reminding me to put a bandage on my thumb before hitting balls rather than after the damage was done. From then on, I had a roll of white first-aid tape in my bag — my thumb and fourth finger of my left hand were always taped because the skin on my hands and feet were — then and now — like papier-mâché.

Another reading assignment came in the form of *Thirty Years of Championship Golf* by Gene Sarazen with Herbert Warren Wind. More structured than the Snead book, it was again underlined by Mr. Pulver with emphasis on fundamentals and mechanics but also with a note that he had been at Fresh Meadow in Queens when Sarazen won the U.S. Open in 1932. There was also a note made in a margin later in the book about a 1926 match in Florida between Bob Jones and Walter Hagen. Mr. Pulver bet $50 on Hagen to win and he "administered a decisive lacing to Bob." That was a big-money bet in those days! I can just see him at these events, soaking it all in as I did from him nearly 60 years later. This also must have been an enormously important book for Mr. Pulver because he would resend it to me in October 1984 when I was a sophomore in college.

Mr. Pulver was truly a fan and student of the game, not just the men's game. He was equally learned about the women's game and the "Super Greats" of both, as

Gene Sarazen helps New York State Women's Amateur Champion Helen Hicks master a shot from a sloping lie. Photo courtesy of New York State Golf Association.

"One may go back in many ways, but must approach the ball from the INSIDE, coming down. This is the most important thing which I have learned after sixty years of golf." — George Pulver

June 11, 1982

DOTTIE:

In my lifetime, I would chronicle the Super great
players to be:

Bobby Jones,	Glenna Collett,
Walter Hagen,	Van Wie,
Gene Sarazen,	Rawls,
Tommy Armour,	Berg,
Sam Snead,	Weathered,
Nelson,	Carner,
Trevino	Smith,
Nichlaus	
Palmer	

Of course, there were a great number of wonderful players,
crowding the super players, but the super players had
something which kept them a notch ahead of the pack.

That something -- not their physiques, certainly not
their swings, and indeed not their intellect. That
something in my view was the unyielding desire to win.
To the very end, to do the very best that they can, in
spite of any set-backs which may be thrust upon them. Not
an easy assignment, but one faced by all those who would
reach for the top in any field.

PLEASE READ CAREFULLY THIS SARAZEN BOOK! RETURN IT AT
YOUR LEISURE. The matches, not the pleasantries and frills,
deserve a focus.

Finally, as Snead has remarked: "The Sun does not shine on the
same dog all the time." One must recognized, that they shall
lose some, as win some, but hang in there!

Miss Dottie Pepper,   George Pulver, Sr.
Box 191,   Geo
Worth Road,
Gansevoort, N. Y. 12831.

he called them, emphasizing their "unyielding desire to win." That has not changed — there are players, there are winners, and there are champions, but the "Super Greats" are in another column because of that desire and nonstop pursuit of winning. With all of the money and material gains available in professional golf (many professional sports, for that matter), it's easy to settle for less. "Super Greats" never settle.

Pepper wins Junior title

GUILDERLAND — The PGA Junior Golf Championships, held this year at Pinehaven Country Club, had the same result in the girls division for the third consecutive time around.

Dottie Pepper of McGregor Links Country Club won the event for the third straight year as she shot a four-over-par 76 to capture the title by seven strokes. Her closest rival was Ballston Spa's Nancy Ryan, who came in with an 83.

The 16-year-old Pepper, who had one birdie and parred 14 other holes, now qualifies for PGA Junior Nationals which will be held at the PGA National Golf Course at Palm Beach Gardens, Fla. on August 19-22.

Clipping from the Saratogian.

Even though I was knocked out in the opening round defending my Women's State Amateur title, the Men's State Amateur was soon to be staged at McGregor, and the official program put great emphasis on me being a McGregor member and my relationship with Mr. Pulver since he was such an enormous part of the club for nearly four decades. Mr. Pulver's desire to remain in the background was never-ending.

As the prospect of this book became a reality, his daughter Madelyn said to me, "He would be so embarrassed" to be such a focus. My response was, "Good, we're going to do just that!"

This July 28 letter is a second version of the original, since he chides himself for being so "bumbling." He must have thought after mailing the original that he was too wordy,

July 28, 1982

Miss Dottie Pepper
Worth Road,
Box 191
Gansevoort, N. Y, 12831

Dottie:

I do, indeed appreciate the McGregor Program. The nostalgia, and even the
re-run of forty years of fighting the inhospitable sands of Wilton, unroll
before my eyes.

Of course, I hasten to thank you for your kind remarks, in which my name was
mentioned. The very first time that I worked with you, I recognized your
talent, your desire, and your power.

My help, I consider marginal, yet I felt that I could give you the distillation
of sixty years of golf, as a golf pro. Some benefits may surface, that would
abet your natural gifts. From time to time I may throw suggestion at you --
try them out in the crucible of actual play -- should they do no good abandom
them after trial.

FIRMER WRISTS IN YOUR PUTTING. We are thinking of short putts and fast greens.
The back swing should be reduced, but not the forward half. You may find it
wise to alter your putting grip (left hand slightly more to the left --right
hand slightly more to the right). This tends to eliminate the opening of the
club head going back, and the closing of the club head going through.

PROGRAMING SETTING UP TO THE BALL IN THE ADDRESS. Your present programing
is excellent, but try to habit the same time span in getting the ball away.
Yes, for the important shots as well as the casual ones. Here your temperment
enters, but make it uniform.

Looking-up on short putts on fast greens is a monster that grows on everyone,
as your peripheral vision catches sight of the hole peeping at them.

Learn to set the club face with both hads as you step to the ball. This is
superior and more natural than setting with either hand, and preserves and
aligns your shoulder line at the same time.

Please pass along a word of cheer to your father and mother.

Geo. Pulver.

P. S.) I am so deeply moved by your annotation on the Sirianna article,
I feel inadequate to respond.

Looking-up on short putts on fast greens is a monster that grows on everyone,
as your peripheral vision catches sight of the hole peeping at them.

too flowery, perhaps feeling like he wasn't his usual, direct self. I must have followed orders in disposing of the original, but it couldn't possibly have been that bad. In the letter, Mr. Pulver was reticent to make any claim to my success. His help, he said, "I consider marginal." As usual, he undersold himself.

I would go on to lose later that week in the final of the State Girls Junior to Kellie Stenzel. Kellie would become a teammate at Furman — a grinder who left it all on the course every day. I simply underestimated her and her game. I came in too cocky and resting on my record. It was a tough lesson to learn but good to learn it early. Again, however, the Pulver look was always forward, with a balance of mind and body, prepared for a reset.

July 31, 1982

Miss Dottie Pepper,
Box 191, Worth Road,
Gansevoort, N. Y.

Dottie:

Thank you for calling.

Of course, you must have felt let down! The words of Hemmingway come to mind. "Generations may come and generations may go, but the old world keeps on turning, and the Sun still rises."

Put away those golf clubs for a few days, until compulsion drives you back. Laugh, be happy, have fun. Your mind has taken the real punishment, not your body.

You have had a fantastic two years of golf successes for one so young. Sadly but surely you shall learn you shall lose some matches. There would be no just God in the sky, should his smiles fall only on the few.

Down the road, I predict many accolades shall come to your skills.

It will be nice to see you Saturday.

George J. Pulver.

Geo

"Put away those golf clubs for a few days, until compulsion drives you back. Laugh, be happy, have fun. Your mind has taken the real punishment, not your body." — George Pulver

August 28, 1982

Miss Dottie Pepper,
Werth Road,
Box 191
Gansevoort, N. Y.

Dottie:

Your golf remains superlative. You may be impatient, but your golf is unfolding
as it should.

This Mrs. Baker has turned you back two years, but she must be rapidly running
our of successes. On the other hand, years of acclaim lie before you. She
is a member of Willows, and no doubt often plays nearby Edison, and is closely
attuned to the grass surfaces.

The tale of Robert Bruce, heroic Scottish King, who won independence from England,
comes to mind: Three times he assailed the English armies, and three times his
brave Scots were driven from the field of battle. Lonely, discomforted, Bruce
found himself in a cave. As he sat there with his melancholy, he observed a
Spider, swinging back and forth trying to reach the safety of his nest. Three
valiant efforts failed, but in his fourth attempt, the Spider reached his nest.
The story goes, Bruce arose, buckle on his sword, and gathered his scattered
minions together. Returning to battle, drove the English from the field.

If you are available next year march right back to that Gazette event, and give
it your best -- your moment may be just around the corner.

HANG IN THERE!

A word of cheer to your father and mother.

George

That reset had me finishing second in the PGA Junior at Palm Beach Gardens, albeit a distant 10 shots behind Heather Farr, unquestionably the best female junior player in the country. It also had me beaten again in the Gazette Women's Amateur. Alice Baker had my number. Bummed? Big time.

Again, Mr. Pulver came up with a winner in the tale of the Scottish king, Robert Bruce, and the king's dogged determination to win independence from England. It not only helped me set an early goal of winning the Gazette event the next year but also achieving something that I'd been denied five times before: qualifying to be the first female in the New York State High School Championship.

I'm proud to have played a part in girls golf becoming a reality in New York State Section II athletics, because until 2019, there was no Section Championship that would serve as a qualifier for the girls' state high school championship. It seems archaic but it was true. I played all of my scholastic golf — six years in total — on the boys team at Saratoga Springs High School because there was no team for girls.

There were so many dedicated educators, PGA professionals, administrators, parents and volunteers involved in finally having more girls teams in the area and of high enough quality to warrant a section championship in 2019 — yes, 36 years after I made it to the championship at Cornell — as the qualifier for a girls statewide championship.

Dottie with two of the participants in the inaugural Section II Girls Golf Championship. Photo courtesy of Tracie Warner, NENY PGA

By October, I knew I needed a new set of clubs. I had become too strong for my current set and it was time to match equipment with strength. Back then, it wasn't the science that it is today. No high-speed cameras, launch monitors, pressure plates or any other of today's tech advantages.

"On the other hand, years of acclaim lie before you." — George Pulver

Mr. Pulver had a work shed behind his house that was simply amazing. As someone who built his own branded hickory clubs, he continued to fiddle in that shed with all that was available at the time. Anytime I could stick my nose in there was priceless. Imagine Arnold Palmer's workshop in Latrobe, Pennsylvania, reduced by about 80 percent: that was this little shed, stuffed full of golf history while still being current.

Mr. Pulver at work in the McGregor Links shop.

Mr. Pulver's shed, where equipment magic happened.
Photo courtesy of David and Allison Meyers

His expertise showed through in this letter, where he discusses the importance and intricacies of a club's shaft.

Mr. Pulver's feel for a swing weight (he equated one swing weight to that of a dollar bill) was, in music terms, pitch perfect. He taught me what that feel was by closing my eyes with various clubs in my hands. Such a gift.

"… by the time you are twenty-five, you may have to change sets several times, in order to match your increased strength and dexterity." — George Pulver

October 3, 1982

Miss Dottie Pepper
Box 191, Worth Road,
Gansevoort N. Y. 12831

Dottie:

On Saturday, I was happy to see your swing fundamentals remain. Be most
careful to make radical   swing changes. Your swing has carried you far.
Already, your swing fits your body, and it is not contrived. It is very
good. Of course, slight changes shall come with the years, but your present
method of attacking a golf ball should not be discarded. Embellished, improved, Yes!

Now fitting you to another set of golf clubs is quite another matter. In
fact by the time you are twenty-five, you may have to change sets several
times, in order to match your increased strength and dexterity.

A golf club shaft is perhaps the most complex component in the entire club.
There are definite guide lines one must follow in this search. Clearly one
must experiment with different types of shafts and weights. Only by hitting
balls can one determine what works best for them. The flight and feel, should
be your guide. The following rules may help:

<u>A shaft is too stiff</u>, if one gets consistantly low shots. An unsolid feeling
at impact on all but centered hits. A pattern of pushes and slices, and working hard to move the ball.
<u>A shaft is too weak,</u> if your shots are mostly high shots --a whippy feeling --
or excessive hooking.

Having said that, I would urge you not to rush into a change. You may have
an opportunity to examine, even to hit a few shots with some of your good
playing girl friends clubs. as you travel about.

I have a few odd clubs, I would like to see you hit with at the range in the
near future. Only as a lead to your ultimate choice.

Say hello to your father and mother, and Jackie:

George Pulver

Sincerely,

Geo

P. S. There is another smaller shaft maker, other than True Temper and
Union Hardware --Accles & Pollard . I thought I saw AP 44 on that club
that the salesman left with you. It may be a medium men's shaft with the
high flex characteristics of the Dynamic. If the salesman represents
Titleist, I wonder where he picked it up. That head is most surely a
MacGregor and I also observed that someone had been tinkering with the
sole plate, perhaps adding or taking away lead? SEE YOU, SUNDAY, OCT. 10Th.

1:30 PM

The arrival of fall golf and dropping temperatures prompted Mr. Pulver to weigh in on strategies associated with playing in colder weather. This letter is a gem, a practical reminder of the preparation for and adjustments necessary for cold-weather golf. Note the basics with bits of detail woven in, but always with a big emphasis on the fundamentals and keeping things simple, especially the backswing.

The college selection process continued to play out with a formal visit to Texas Christian University, followed by Furman in South Carolina a week later. Meeting Byron Nelson at Colonial and Ben Hogan at Shady Oaks during that trip to Texas was powerful, and the idea of playing on a stacked team that would win the national championship just months later was phenomenal. But the truth was, Furman was the fit for me. The schools were about the same size, but Furman had its own course and practice facility on campus, while TCU had playing privileges at a few courses in and around Fort Worth. I wouldn't have a car, so that was a big first strike. The second strike against TCU was what I saw the freshmen on the team studying: courses I had already taken or was currently taking in high school. Third was the distance from home: I wanted to spread my wings, but almost 1,700 miles, nearly twice as far as Furman, was just too far. The final nail in the Horned Frog coffin was being told it would take four and a half to five years to get an undergraduate degree. I would be wearing purple and white at either institution, but I decided I would be a Paladin for the next four years. Furman was exactly where I needed to be.

I still have to chuckle when people ask me how a kid from Upstate New York made it to Furman University, then a small Southern Baptist, liberal arts institution in Greenville, South Carolina. I suppose it was part luck, part the powerful Furman network, and part divine intervention that resulted in a letter I wrote in late 1980 to Clemson University's head golf coach, Bobby Robinson, ultimately landing in Willie Miller's in-basket. Willie was the men's and women's coach at Furman. The database at our high school that I used to search out college golf programs was unable to filter men's and women's golf; only golf could be input. At the time Clemson did not offer women's golf, but Coach Robinson, a Furman alum, thought his counterpart 33 miles away might be interested in the letter.

Willie Miller, men's and women's golf coach at Furman
Photo courtesy of Furman University Sports Information Department

Thank you, Coach Robinson!

"When I saw the letter of inquiry and resume that was forwarded to me from Coach Robinson, my first thought was 'she can really play golf and I need her at Furman.'" — Willie Miller

October 14, 1982

Miss Dottie Pepper,
Worth Road,
Box 191
Gansevoort, N. Y. 12831

Dottie:

I met your mother the other day and she reported that you were teeing off
at the Edison at 8:00 A. M. It was chilly hence it got me thinking of cold
weather golf.

No one, and I repeat, no one plays golf quite as well when it is cold, as
when it is warm. Some manage better than others, but all are affected.
First, cold air is denser than warm air, therefore the ball does not go
as far. Then, your touch around the greens are not aided by numb hands,
and layers of clothing. The grass on the greens is stiffer and slower.

Which factor interfears the most? Stiff muscles -- errant judgement of
distances -- layers of clothing. Frankly, I am less than certain. Probably
all are contributing. Now what can be done to lessen these conditions?

It seems to me the hands and wrists should be kept warm, and an extra effort
should be made to get the big muscles working. We are really talking about
the turn of the body on the backswing, minimizing the use of the hands and
wrists.

Always a great aid to this would be to avoid tension in the shoulder area --
start back slowly, and most importantly, GO BACK WITH THE CLUB SHAFT AND
LEFT ARM (ALL IN ONE PIECE) AT LEAST UNTIL THE CLUB HEAD IS ABOUT OPPOSITE
THE RIGHT-HIP. The trouble with cold weather golf, in fact, most bad golf,
one hurries the swing, neglects to adequately turn his shoulders, and uses
his hands and wrists too early and excessively.

AND BY THE WAY -- Starting back slowly all in one piece, is an excellent
manner to embark in moving a golf ball at any time.

Hang in there -- your golf is unfolding as it should. A word to cheer to
your father and mother.

George Pulver.

P. S. Should you get another set of irons, with A shafts, Swt. D --diameter
of your grips small men's or large ladies, I think you will be fitted. And
I would like to observe you hitting a few balls with such a set.

By early November, I updated Mr. Pulver with the details behind my choice of Furman. Looking back on the letter now — and Mr. Pulver's reply — it seems clear that we both recognized that this step into the college game would mean some changes in our relationship.

November 8, 1982

Dear Mr. Pulver:

Hi! Thanks so much for the Furman catalogue that I found in the mailbox this afternoon. Yes, I did have one but an extra copy is always very nice to have.

Regarding my choice of Furman, I feel I should fill you in on a few of the more important details concerning both the academics and the golf program. I have been looking at Furman since I was a freshman in high school and for me, this opportunity is like a dream come true. Although the school is very small, it offers just about anything a person could ever want. The university does not offer a major in communications but, I can design my own major under the supervision of Mr. Charles Brock, the head of the Admissions Department. I will be taking a number of courses in the fields of English, Business, Physical Education, and Communications. As you probably know, for a time I was considering attending Texas Christian University. I chose Furman over TCU because of Furman's "tri-mester" schedule. Under this schedule I will take 3 courses in the fall and the spring while I will be taking only two courses in the winter. There is only one tournament scheduled during the winter term so, during that time, I will concentrate more heavily on my more difficult courses. At TCU the girls are constantly catching up with school work because of a continuous golf schedule. TCU's year is divided up into only two parts. Also, the education process for athletes at TCU takes 4½ - 5 years. At Furman, only four years of college work is required to get a degree.

As for Furman's golf schedule and program, I think very highly of it. They play a top ranked schedule against the best schools in the country, such as Arizona State, TCU, Tulsa, SMU, Florida, and San Jose State. The team plays 10 major collegiate tournaments plus the NCAA Championship, the AIAW Championship and Furman's own collegiate tournament, The Lady Paladin. Practice is held nearly everyday at Furman's own championship course that is right on campus. (The campus is situated on 750 acres of land.) In addition to unlimited use of Furman's course and practice facilities, we also have easy access to 4 other courses in the Greenville area; one of these being Chanticlair, ranked among the top 50 courses in the United States. The coach is wonderful, too. His name is Michel Potter and he is a native of Cortland, N.Y. Coach Potter is a firm believer in fundamentals. I truly believe that by attending Furman, I will be able to advance my academic skills and golf prowess at the same time. I am very excited about going to Furman next fall. I will be coming home for Thanksgiving each year, plus I have a 4 week vacation from the middle of December to the middle of January. Don't worry, you'll be seeing plenty of me during my vacations. Of course, I'll be spending my entire summer at home taking lessons from the greatest pro I know!

Keep in touch and take care.

Love always,

Dottie

P.S. I got a chance to meet Byron Nelson while I was in Texas. He reminded me a lot of you.

November 20, 1982

MISS DOTTIE PEPPER:

Dottie:

My tardy reply to your happy Furman letter of November 8th., and your subsequent Thanksgiving card, can only be ascribed to the fact, I now find "The faster I run, alas, I remain in the same place."

Actually, during the past two weeks, I have had a few chores at Brookhaven-- putting the course in bed for the winter, that come Spring it shall be ready.

My daughter Jean passed by a few weeks ago, returing from France where she chaperoned a group of Seniors, attending Sorbonne University in Paris. After the four weeks school thing, Jean's husband came over, and they hired a car and toured a number of Scottish golf courses. Of course, they set no records, but Jean especially favors St. Andrews, Turnberry, and Glen Eagles.

It was she who mailed me Furman's catalogue from her office in Atlanta. She spoke of the school with the same enthusiasm as you did. She reports that the school shall not overpower you -- the campus magnificient, and its academic excellence, unchangeable. Further! It is not too far away.

All the reasons which impelled you to choose Furman makes sense to me as a father as well as a golf pro. Your majors and electives appear to be wisely chos Of course, you will have to put in many hours bumping balls to keep up with your peers. In the meantime, you show great sagacity in determining to not neglect your academics as well.

You must know I shall be ever ready to work with you. How long my limited golf knowledge shall be able to match your experience remains to be seen, but it is my hope, my little bit, somehow help your golf to advance.

Say hello to your Father and Mother. Please include Jackie.

Sincerely,

George J. Pulver.

There is a delicate balance to be struck when a young player leaves for college to work with coaches whose philosophies about the game and teaching may be different from what she learned at home. This has not changed in the nearly 40 years since I made that transition. I believe the balance is a bit easier today because video can be shared instantly with the player's personal coach. But college coaches need to be able to use their skills to get the best from each of their players, and ultimately their team, without the anxiety of overstepping into another teacher's territory. Can this be awkward? Yes. Is it a conversation that must happen for everyone's benefit?

"How long my limited golf knowledge shall be able to match your experience remains to be seen, but it is my hope, my little bit, somehow may help your golf to advance." — George Pulver

November 24, 1982

Dear Mr. Pulver;

Thanks so much for your letter of November 20 and your letter from your daughter, Jean. It always such a joy to hear from you.

I have recently been thinking about the number of colleges and universities that I was recruited by. I never thought it would number this many:

Furman University
Texas Christian University
University of South Florida
Wake Forest University
University of Arizona
Arizona State University
University of Tulsa
Penn State University

Perhaps through the winter months there will be a few more. But, I truly feel I made my wisest decision in choosing Furman over the rest. The school's record, both in golf and academics, speaks for itself.

I have also been thinking about this past golf season. At times I played remarkable golf. 3 of the 4 rounds that I played at the PGA National Juniors were the best I have ever played. My consistency throughout those rounds astonished even myself. But at other times, I led myself to believe that I could perhaps become victorious on my past victories. I now know that in this strange game, only the present time counts. At the Sports Dinner at the Empire State Plaza last Friday night, Digger Phelps, the basketball coach at the University of Notre Dame, spoke at great length about scholastics and athletics. Physchologically, Coach Phelps was a great help to me. He commented on never trying to win on your past performances. I learned a great deal from that. I truly believe that the days that I played less than acceptable golf, I was playing on my past merits- expecting the magic of last season to somehow come alive again. Next year will be totally be different. This year I practiced more than ever but it always seemed that the spark or something else was missing once in a while. I am so excited about this up coming season. By qualifying for the boy's state high school championship, which was one of my pre- season goals, my confidence and enthusiasm has been fully renewed.

Please keep in touch.
My best wishes to Madelyn and Jean.

Love -
Dottie

Jean
please mail
back to me!
Pass hello to mel
Love
Dad

PS We all had a good dinner. Madelyn is not only an excellent business person, but she excels as a cook.
Dad

Yes again. I would, of course, have a coach in college and Mr. Pulver would be less hands-on in the week-to-week evolution of me and my game, but that would not strain our relationship.

On the day before Thanksgiving, I thanked Mr. Pulver for his continued encouragement and was relieved to see that he was pleased with my choice. I took the opportunity to reflect on a year that seemed to have a lot more lows than highs — a personal reckoning with relying too much on past performance and an awareness of how important it is to make practice quality time over quantity. I had spent a lot of time practicing but, truthfully, it wasn't of the quality it should have been. The Digger Phelps speech in Albany really hit home and what a small world this truly is: I would be seated behind Digger and his wife at the Houston funeral of President H.W. Bush in December 2018.

```
December 11, 1092

MISS DOTTIE PEPPER,
GANSEVOORT, N. Y.

DOTTIE:

I hasten to join your many admirers in congratulations.  I refer
to your continuation of making the first honor roll in your final
year at Saratoga High.

Continue to seek excellence and good health in all of your efforts.
Whatever peerless athletic skills one may possess, it is prudent to
march them side by side with cerebral ones, as well.

Whatever one's field -- those who rise just a notch a above their peers,
are the ones who not only sweat, but think, also.  Or, at least, it seems
to me.

Merry Christmas, and say hello to your father and mother.  Please, do
not bother to respond.

Sincerely,

George J. Pulver.
```

As the year wound down, Mr. Pulver offered another reminder of how much he valued education and how in tune he was with our city through the local newspaper. I achieved Honor Roll at Saratoga Springs High School for the first half of the senior year, even with a college scholarship in hand, and that did not go unnoticed with Mr. Pulver. All three of his children were college-educated, but he also believed that learning was a journey without end.

"I truly believe that the days that I played less than acceptable golf, I was playing on my past merits — expecting the magic of last season to somehow come alive again." — *Dottie Pepper*

December 23, 1982

MISS DOTTIE PEPPER:

DOTTIE::

After you left, I gave some thought to pitching problems. I must add that
every first class golfer sooner or later must face such a problem. You may
two wedges -- one less heavy and lighter shafted than the other. At this point,
we are talking about shots from grass rather than sand.

Hogan and Revolta could play these shots with great wrist action--their balls
would come out hot, and pull back as they hit the green. On the other hand,
Snead and Venturi, tossed these shots up with a slow, mostly arm action--the
ball was dropped short of the pin, and rolled about fifteen feet. Hogan and
Revolta played the ball from slightly back in their stance, rather than from
nearer the middle.

One should try both types of shots, but I am tilted towards the slow, floating
style to be best for most people. Yet if one has the touch and genious of a Hogan
or Revolta, they should go with whatx they have.

As you play with your peers, observe the ones who seem to be masters of this short
pitch from grass. Look into their bags -- even gain permission to hit a few shots
with their favorite wedge. Money is not the answer. One is as likely to come
across a fitting wedge from an old barrel of discards. Such a wedge should be
heavier than the usual family of irons, but not as heavy as some sand wedges, and
be shafted with a lighter shaft.

Many of the foremost women players play this shot as well as the leading men
pros. I use men as an example, only because I have observed men more.

Be concerned, but don't fret too much! This shot will come! Certainly three
clubs must be mastered --Driver, Wedges, and Putter.

MERRY CHRISTMAS AND HAPPY NEW YEAR TO YOU AND YOUR PARENTS.

George J. Pulver.

Geo

With just a few days left before Christmas, Mr. Pulver turned his attention to pitching problems. If there was one thing I struggled with over the course of my career, it was pitching. So the letter was a welcomed way to end the year with more teaching and the prospect of the winter months to work on it.

I love how he presented two different ways of tackling the issue, with detailed descriptions of both as well as professional examples. I could see those players in my mind's eye and the feel of what he was describing in my hands. I still believe that when a teacher can make this come together — see it, feel it — magic happens.

Dottie at the 1998 Solheim Cup. Muirfield Village Golf Club. Dublin, Ohio. Photo courtesy of the Solheim Cup.

"I am tilted towards the slow, floating style (of chipping) to be the best for most people. Yet if one has the touch and genius of a Hogan or Revelta, they should go with what they have." — George Pulver

I dabbled in free verse poetry as a kid. One example is a piece I wrote during the 1980 Winter Olympics in nearby Lake Placid. I was totally mesmerized by the Games and the stories of how the athletes paid such prices to become Olympians. This piece hangs in my office today as an overlay on a photo of Brandie Burton and me waving a large American flag after we both went undefeated in the 1994 Solheim Cup at the Greenbrier in West Virginia.

QUEST

Fight, Win, Be #1
A non-stop quest for sports immortality
Dedication – the main ingredient
The long march has just begun with your first step

"Push yourself" – it's a quote often heard
Push, push, push
Years of constant struggle, pain, tears
Disappointments and elations

All part of the price
Don't stop now – the gold medal is within sight
Within your reach
Don't quit now – the impossible trek is coming to an end

The crowd roars
The ovation starts
Louder, louder, louder
Your country's flag waving in the victorious breeze

One more step
The greatest of all
The middle stand
Gold upon your breast

— *Dottie Pepper, age 14*

How different that tone was two years later as I realized what I had, how perceptions had changed both internally and externally, and how much I wanted to get back on top. But first, it was on to Furman.

BEING NUMBER ONE

By Dottie Pepper 182

In the past year I realized that it's really
        not easy being Number One.
I thought that once I had attained that envious
        spot, things would be much easier.
In fact, I totally enjoyed being Number One until
        I realized I was no longer the underdog.
I had spent three years as an underdog-
        a contender but not a proven winner.
Then suddenly I was the player to beat-
        "The Kid."
The notoriety was wonderful at first-
        but then the pressure began to set in.
Suddenly I had everything to lose-
        and I lost it.
Just as quickly a I became Number One,
        I had lost that prestigious ranking.
I learned a great deal from my descending experience.
Now I must start all over again.
Perhaps this time I will stay on the crescent
        of that tall, steep mountain peak.

Photos courtesy of Special Collections and Archives, James B. Duke Library, Furman University.

"... I truly feel I made the wisest decision in choosing Furman over the rest. The school's record, both in golf and academics, speaks for itself." — Dottie Pepper

TOURNAMENT RECORD

1982 - (Age 16-17)

- Failed to qualify, LPGA Corning Classic, Corning C.C.

- Winner, Northeastern Golf Association, McGregor Links

- Winner, New York State Amateur Sponsors Tournament, McGregor Links

- Winner, Northeastern Women's Golf Association Gail Sykes Best Ball Championship, Pinehaven C.C.

- Winner, PGA National Junior Championship Qualifier, Pinehaven C.C.

- Lost first round, New York State Women's Amateur Championship, Ives Hill C.C.

- Lost in final round, New York State Junior Girls Championship, The Pompey Club

- Winner, Northeastern Junior Girls Championship, Cordial Greens C.C.

- 6th place tie, Dr. Jack Spitalny Memorial Junior Tournament, Colonie C.C.

- 2nd place, PGA National Junior Championship, The Champion Course

- 2nd place, Gazette Women's Amateur Championship, The Edison Club

- Winner, McGregor Links C.C. Women's Club Championship

- Winner, Schenectady Golf Association Falling Leaves Championship, Schenectady Municipal G.C.

Chapter 4 *"Today we plan and work for the accolades of tomorrow."*

Mr. Pulver continued to write over the winter of 1983, including sharing articles from the most recent golf publications, with key people and topics usually underlined. His off-season emphasis in these letters focused on building a reservoir of determination

GEORGE J. PULVER
136 EAST AVENUE
SARATOGA SPRINGS, NEW YORK 12866

January 11, 1983

MISS DOTTIE PEPPER
Box 196,
Worth Road,
Gansevoort, N. Y. 12831

DOTTIE:

I join your many friends in congratulations. I refer,
of course, to your Jordan interview, which appeared in
The Saratogian, as of January 10th.

It would be difficult to fault your ambition or direction.
Your scenario looks good. Try to stick with it.

Sponge-up all you can in education. Choose carefully your
majors. Of course, Golf must become No. 1, but not entirely.

Please re-read Watson's article appearing in current Golf
Digest. To be a champion, one must not only be a great striker
of a golf ball, but he also must possess wisdom, determination,
and the will to "Hang in There." I have always felt that champions
in any field, to remain a notch or so ahead of their peers,
have a superior cerebral quality to think.

With every good wish. Today, we plan and work for the accolades
of tomorrow.

George.
Leo

P. S. Jean, one of my daughters sent me several boxes of this
flossy paper. This seemed a good moment to start using some of
it. Please, do not bother to respond.

— what would be an often-used term by him, the will to "hang in there," in this case as displayed by Tom Watson.

With my college commitment now made and that hurdle cleared, the next eight months were really about putting in the planning and work to finish off my junior golf career with as many good showings and wins as possible while slowly moving more into women's amateur competitions as they were available.

The previous year had been an eye opener, and I was determined not to continue its disappointments, particularly on the local and state level. I worked hard over the winter, often running on the high school track during lunch period and spending extra time in the gym with great support from the teachers and coaches in the physical education department. This season was going to be better!

Without super deep pockets, the rule for putting together a tournament schedule was essentially this: If I could drive, I could play. I needed to get a bit lucky with the upcoming schedules for the state, national, and junior golf associations, and I certainty did. I had qualified for the state high school championship at Cornell already but the American Junior Golf Association (AJGA) was coming to Stratton Mountain, Vermont, just 90 minutes away, and the United States Golf Association (USGA) was bringing two national championships to New Jersey just three hours away. Big-time competitions practically on my doorstep!

Golf Team

ROW ONE: J. Parish, D. Harmon, M. Naughton, T. Sanford, B. Matsik ROW TWO: D. Pepper, M. Gerber, B. Smith, M. Ripple, M. McRoberts, P. Klein, M. Lechevet, Coach J. M. Caldaro Not Pictured: S. Cohan, M. Campola

The '82-'83 Saratoga Springs High School golf team. Shot from the "Recorder," the SSHS yearbook.

January 19, 1983

Dear Mr. Pulver;

Hi. Thanks so much for the note of January 3 and the following
articles of Floyd and Watson. They proved to be very enjoyable
reading with a great deal to be learned from both of them also.

I find myself at home with some type of a virus right now. Hope-
fully, it will pass soon.

Other than that, everything is going well around here. The snow
has been a real blessing for the ski industry. I am definitely
looking forward to the golf season, though. My new clubs should
be here in approximately six weeks.

Dad and I have been carefully planning my tournament schedule for
the summer. It seems to be coming around well. There are still
a couple of unsettling flaws in it, but they should be worked out
within the next month. This is how it is shaping up:

MAY
16- LPGA Corning Classic Amateur Qualifier
        Corning CC, Corning, N.Y.

26-29- LPGA Corning Classic
        Corning CC, Corning, N.Y.

JUNE
3-6- NYS Boys' State High School Championship
        Cornell U. Golf Course, Ithaca, N.Y.

20-23- American Junior Golf Association Northern Junior Classic
        Stratton Mountain Resort, Stratton, Vermont

24- Graduation: Saratoga Springs High School

28- Gail Sykes Best Ball Championship
        Oneonta CC, Oneonta, N.Y.

JULY
5-6- Gazette Women's Amateur Championship
        The Willows CC, Rexford, N.Y.

12-17- NYS Women's Amateur Championship
        Seven Oaks CC- Colgate University   (dates still
        Hamilton, N.Y. (Utica area)   tentative)

26-29- NYS Junior Girls Championship
        McConnellsville CC, McConnellsville, N.Y.
        (Rome area)   (dates still
                                                    tentative)

AUGUST
8-13 United States Golf Association Junior Girls Championship
        Somerset Hills CC, Bernardsville, NJ

15-20- United States Golf Association Women's Amateur Ch.
        Canoe Brook CC, Summit, NJ

22-26- New England Junior Open
        Ponkapoeg GC, Canton, Mass. (Boston area) ....

t this point, it looks like I will pass up the US Women's Amateur and play in the Northeast Junior Open instead. The main reason for this choice is the dates and sites of the qualifying rounds for the national championship. My state championships hold a high spot on the list of priorities for this summer. After losing both of the titles last summer, I am particularly hungry for them this year. I won't sacrifice a state championship to qualify for the nationals. I don't really think I am at the point to win the US Amateur, anyway. I'm sure the Northeast Junior Open will be a good place to finish out my junior career.

Well, I guess I should be going. I should try to get some sleep and catch up on some school work. Thanks again for the mail and we'll hope for an early and warm srping. We've got our work cut out for us this year.

Best Wishes -
Dottie

Note my enthusiastic but still cautiously realistic tone at the end of this letter to Mr. Pulver. His homespun, home-won philosophy — that is, finding wins near home vs. far away — was definitely taking up residence in my thinking and planning.

In the first paragraph of this letter, I referenced two articles that Mr. Pulver had sent me on Jan. 3, along with a handwritten note. The articles were on Raymond Floyd and Watson, two of the greatest grinders the game has ever known. Floyd had a stare and focus that was unmistakable, and when my "grind mode" would later be compared to his, it was just about the highest compliment I could have been given.

What is Tom Watson Driving at?

*With Ben Hogan's top half, Jack Nicklaus's
bottom half, and plenty of guts,
Watson has become the world's greatest golfer.*
by David Owen

It is possible to wonder why sensible people play golf. The golf swing is one of the most complex and unnatural movements in all of sports. Its plane of motion slices through the body at an awkward angle, neither parallel nor perpendicular to the golfer's stance. Turning the hip a fraction of a second too soon or a few degrees in the wrong direction can send the ball careering out of bounds. A slight misplacement of the thumb can destroy any shot. When a golfer finds he is having trouble with his game, he begins to worry about things like the thickness of his socks.

One measure of a sport's inherent difficulty is the amount of lying it provokes in the people who play it casually. A man continually baffled and humiliated by a game he plays for relaxation will soon begin to lie about it, and weekend golfers are the most notorious liars of all. One of the great clubhouse jokes involves a golfer so used to cheating that when he makes a hole in one, he marks it on his scorecard as a zero.

If it's hard to imagine playing golf in the first place, it's nearly impossible to conceive of playing it for a living. The odds against a talented young golfer's making a name for himself as a pro are almost incalculable. Even if he manages to earn his tour card from the Professional Golfers' Association (about one chance in twenty on his first try) and then qualify for a tournament (roughly one chance in ten any given week), he still faces the challenge of playing well enough over the first two days to be allowed to remain in the competition. Players who don't make the cut don't earn a cent. Merely meeting expenses on the tour requires winning a minimum of twenty-five thousand dollars, something 139 card-carrying pros

Photographs, *left and right:* John Iacono/Sports Illustrated; *center,* Focus on Sports; *opposite,* Bonnie Schiffman, courtesy of Esquire Magazine

The Watson article had originally come from Madelyn to her dad, but he thought that the lengthy *Esquire* piece would be a good read for me. He was right again. David Owen's in-depth look at Watson's beginnings in the game, his genuine love of golf, his participation in other sports as a kid, going to college for four years, the decision to eventually turn professional, playing on a lean budget — these were all topics Mr. Pulver and I had spent time discussing and applying to my own situation. But the biggest takeaway from the article for me was Watson's unrelenting desire to win when most of the galleries were cheering for Jack Nicklaus. And what really stuck was Hubert Green's quote in the piece saying in reference to Watson, "He's got a garbage-can full of guts." That's the kind of player I wanted to be.

A huge opportunity to get the year going in the right direction would come at the top of the spring schedule, a second chance to enter the amateur qualifier for the LPGA Corning Classic. I had that opportunity a year before as the reigning women's state amateur champion, but I didn't make it. After failing in that 1982 qualifier, I convinced Mom and Dad that I should go back to the tournament itself two weeks later as a volunteer standard bearer, staying with friends I had made playing in the state junior tournaments. But my parents decided it was too far to drive by myself, so I took the Greyhound bus from nearby Schenectady to Corning and back. When you've got a dream, you chase it any way possible. That experience reinforced my desire to play professional golf and only made me want to qualify more when I would get this second chance in early 1983.

How ironic that I write this book sharing the years of correspondence, wisdom, and mentorship of Mr. Pulver while the Covid-19 pandemic has affected nearly every bit of daily life and movement we took for granted just months ago. I had gotten sick with some sort of virus when I wrote him in mid-January that year, but coming from one who not only survived the time of the Spanish Flu and being injured and gassed in World War I, he was right: "it shall pass."

A substantial March thaw meant a bonus day at the range with Mr. Pulver. He had given me one of Madelyn's sand wedges to work with over the winter, a Wilson R-90. The better tool allowed more experimentation and creativity. His belief in exposing players to all sorts of equipment and feels was playing out again: Try different things and learn what works best for you.

GEORGE J. PULVER
136 EAST AVENUE
SARATOGA SPRINGS, NEW YORK 12866

Miss Dottie Pepper,
Box 196,
Gansevoort, N. Y. 12831

Dottie:

I was sorry to learn that you were having a go with some virus.
My years have forced me to learn, this to be the burden of all
humans. But, I have also learned, it shall pass.

Your schedule looks good to me. You and your father show great wisdom
at looking close to home for contests. Often promising youngsters are
persuaded to go trapping about the country, only because of a well-heel
parent, and by the way an over zealous one as well.

In all games tension surfaces, *as Golf.* but in my view no game, bears down
with such force, First of all, you and your parents should agree in
the amount of peer pressure you should be exposed to, at this point
in time.

In my view, you have the ability with golf, but first you must not
be permitted to burn-out. You must face wins and also losses. These,
so the coaches say, "Are the wages that must be payed." But you shall
be learning.

in athletics, some may leap from obscurity --but not many.Most must
make their way upwards, slowly. Golf can be good to one, yet Golf
and Education, can be surer.

Say hello, to your father and Mother.

George Pulver, Sr.,

Over the winter my schedule continued to evolve, rounding into shape by late March. So I updated Mr. Pulver with this letter listing the tournaments ahead.

March 27, 1983

Dear Mr. Pulver—

Hi! I meant to give you my finalized 1983 tournament schedule this afternoon, but, of course, I forgot! I've got a stiff schedule planned out, but with plenty of work and positive thinking, I believe it will be very successful.

It was a real pleasure to meet your family. They are all truly a credit to you.

Now that we have some snow on the ground again, I'll go back to working on my game inside. I noticed that my lagging on the long putts was horrible. Now I know what I really have to work on. I was charging the long ones like Tom Watson (but I didn't exactly make all of the ones coming back!) I was making good contact with all of my putts—all I need is a little work on the touch!

Overall, I was extremely pleased with my ball striking during the past 2 days—everything was just a little draw or straight. I'm very anxious to get my new irons and driver this week, though. That R-90 sand wedge is fantastic. I practiced with it all winter and now I can do just about anything with it. It seems nice to have confidence with a sand wedge!

Well—I just wanted to be sure you had a copy of my tournament schedule. Hope you had a wonderful birthday and thank-you for a lovely afternoon.

Looking forward to seeing you soon.

Love—
Dottie

"In all games tension surfaces, but in my view no game bears down with such force as golf."
— *George Pulver*

PRESSING MATTERS

1983 Schedule

May 16 - LPGA Corning Classic Qualifier
Corning CC, Corning, NY

May 26-29 - LPGA Corning Classic

June 5-6 : NYS Boys High School Ch.
Cornell U., Ithaca, NY

June 7 - Northeastern Tourney : Colonie CC
June 14 - Northeastern Tourney : Mohawk CC
June 20-23 - AJGA Northern Junior Cl.
Stratton Mtn., Stratton, Vt.

June 24 - Graduation

June 28 - Gail Sykes Best Ball Ch.
Winding Brook CC
Valatie, NY

July 5-6 Gazette Women's Am. Ch.
Willows CC
Rexford, NY

OP0022

July 14-16 - NYS Women's Amateur Ch.
Seven Oak CC
Hamilton, NY (Utica)

July 25-29 - NYS Jr. Girls Ch.
McConnellsville CC
McConnellsville, NY (Rome)

Aug. 2 - Northeastern Tourney - Troy CC

Aug. 8-13 - USE7A Jr. Girls Ch.
Somerset Hills CC
Bernardville, NJ

Aug. 22-26 - New England Jr. Open
Ponkapoag GC
Canton, Mass.

Aug. 30 - Northeastern Tourney - Albany CC

Sept. 7 - Report to Furman U.

Nov. 24-27 - AJGA American Jr. Classic
Innisbrook Resort
Tarpon Springs, Fla.

Mr. Pulver immediately responded, emphasizing the need for a simple approach to putting, one that would not break down under the weight of competition.

He was a firm believer in understanding how varied weather conditions can affect your body and how that can impact preparation and expectations. He also stressed that I would be best served to have a right-to-left ball flight but also an ability to move it the other direction when necessary.

"The present day tournament greens are lightning fast, with devious rolls. Use almost dead wrist, but relaxed, and take the club back SLOWLY. Treat with suspect my advice — I am a lousy putter." — George Pulver

March 30, 1983

Miss Dottie Pepper,
Box 196 Worth Road,
Gansevoort, N. Y. 12813

Dottie:

I was delighted that you, your sister, and your father came by on
Sunday. I was also pleased that you could meet my clan.

In your note, you were kind enough to mention my family. However,
I can claim little credit. This, rightly belongs to their wonderful
mother. As they gather about me, I observe her strong genetic influence.
Really, my role has been an incidental biological one.

Your schedule embraces an ample area of courses and terrain, to say nothing
of the formidable peers you will most surely face. In this moment of your
golf you need look no further, to sharpen your skills.

NOW YOUR GAME -- Being a cautious person, it seem to me that trying to
lag a putt that it will die near the hole, generly will be found to be
the most rewarding. The present day tournament greens are lightning fast,
with devious rolls. Use almost dead wrist, but relaxed, and take the club
back SLOWLY. Treat with suspect my advice -- I am a lousy putter.

Refrain from hitting too many long shots until the weather becomes warmer,
and your muscles are prepared. I am sure that your father can tell you a
few things that cold weather can do to your muscles.

I still feel confident that most men and probably all women, should bring
the ball in slightly from the right on all long shots to get the most out
of their power. Yet infreaqently you will find the need of a slight fade
as so many greens are set-up to come in from the left.

SAND WEDGES -- One day you may find the need of two wedges, to meet the challenges
of mounds and sand found around so many courses today. The Sarazen wedge is
not the best wedge, but it is a good one. It weights about 3 ounces less than
many of the wedges sold today.

At your discretion, I look forward to seeing you bump a few balls some nice
warm day. Please say hello to your family.

George J. Pulver,

I still chuckle when I read his self-deprecating quips throughout the letters, calling his influence on his family more of Martha's "strong genetic influence" than his "incidental biological one," or to be suspect of his input on putting because he was "a lousy putter."

He may not have thought much of his influence, but it was always mindful and practical. One of his best bits of advice was to do everyday things around the house and at work — mindless things like picking up a fork, opening a cabinet or door, grabbing a bag of groceries, walking the dog — with your non-dominant hand so it builds balance and stability on both sides of your body. I am right-hand dominant, but I can confidently eat a formal meal with my left hand. To this day, I still make a habit of doing tasks as much left-handed as I can. Back then, it was common sense; today, it's proved a lifelong reminder of his influence on my life.

Mr. Pulver was not only advising me on how I could keep a well-balanced physical makeup, but, perhaps more important, he guided me on keeping a balanced teenaged life. He was keenly aware of the emotional and psychological toll that can be exacted on kids who show athletic promise.

In what was one of his most pointed letters, he made it very clear that he was not a fan of the methods employed by such coaches as tennis' Nick Bollettieri, questioning the good that comes from limiting or even removing innocence and fun from childhood in pursuit of athletic achievements.

His third paragraph is especially powerful, cautioning of the mental damage that can be inflicted when it is not the child clamoring for more, but a frustrated parent or over-the-top coach incessantly pushing.

Despite his clear warnings and concerns, however, he made a wonderfully positive reference to Chris Evert, making sure I knew that even if I was not the most physically gifted player, the determination to win to the very end was mandatory.

As the Corning qualifier approached, he followed up a lesson with simple thoughts to take to competition, reinforcing the things I was doing well while giving just a few basic thoughts to focus on. Starting the club back slowly, slightly inside, with a square club face … the gold standard. Because a cluttered mind races, he wanted my mind in tournaments to be quiet and slow. Did I always achieve it? Not by any stretch, but these thoughts were planted deeply and permanently.

"In my view, Bollettieri pushes too far. There must be a more humane and thoughtful way to get the most out of young minds and bodies. A tiny few survive by his method — too many are too early crushed."
— George Pulver

April 4, 1983

Miss Dottie Pepper
Box 196, Worth Road,
Gansevoort, N. Y. 12831

Dottie:

The enclosed reader from the Wall Street Journal. This Bollettieri's
article causes me to pause. I am well aware that in sports, indeed all
endevors, if one is to catch the silver ring, they must never, never,
stop trying.

Yet, I ask, must their childhood, their laughter be denied them?
Must they become gnomes, with no dreams or laughter? I say to hell
with all such drivel.

Often, of course, frusterated parents, push their children into an
early and melancholy psychiatric oblivion, in which their precious
youth is actually snatched from them.

Recently Chris Everts said in a television interview. "There are
about twelve women tennis players in the International field, who are
swtronger, more gifted, and possess better games than she does." The
interviewer interrupted -- "How can you say this, for again and again
in world tennis competition, you have beaten these players." After a
thoughtful moment her reply was, "I was determined to win, to the very
end of my matches."

In my view, Bollettieri pushes too far. There must be a more humane
and thoughtful way to get the most out of young minds and bodies. A
tiny few survive by his method -- too many are too early crushed.

Geo J Pulver, Sr.

May 12, 1983

DOTTIE:

It was indeed a pleasure to watch you bang balls into that, cold, inhospitable wind on Tuesday.

There is one suggestion, I would like to repeat. "On the big shots, use a slightly closed stance, and take the club back marginally inside. Keep the club face looking down the flight line."

Your swing is modern in every respect -- On the Upright side, and a great drive of your lower body starting down. I feel that such a swing has evolved from the torsion-free steel shaft.

Seldom do your shots go awry, but when they do the cause, to me, appears to be from a too upright swing arc. SO START YOUR CLUB BACK SLOWLY, AND SLIGHTLY IN! These infrequent shots which may bleed to the right, or pull to the left, could be caused by a slightly too upright, swing plane. I don't mean the peaks.

My enthusiasm for your golf future increases!

GP:
Geo

I did qualify for the LPGA Corning event, and while I ultimately missed the cut, it was his letter of May 19 that held three gems that would be my go-to's throughout my career. The first was, again, his reminder about taking the club back: Do it slowly, almost straight back, with a square club face.

The big addition to that thought was to begin the downswing with the lower body, which is your anchor to the ground and power source. It was super simple, but it spoke to synchronizing the swing's change of direction in a most repeatable, reliable manner.

The last point here is perhaps most important: When the pressure is on, go with the shot you have the most confidence in. It seems so obvious, but when the world starts moving at warp speed during a round, or — to use another metaphor — when the wheels are starting to fall off, it's time to go back to what you know will just get the job done.

"It takes more than a perfect swing to make a champion, and because of musculatures, the best for one, may not be the best for another." — George Pulver

GEORGE J. PULVER
136 EAST AVENUE
SARATOGA SPRINGS, NEW YORK 12866

May 19, 1983

Dottie:

It was nice to see you the other day. As I said
at the time, shooting a 76, on a championship type
course, which is played infrequently, is indeed
note-worthy.

Finally -- Repeating -- start the club back slowly,
almost straight back, keeping the face of the club
looking down the flight line --then as always, lead
with your lower body.

Anytime you find the ball on a slope above the feet --
look for a pull. It is hard to drive the legs in under
such condition. Try aiming slightly right, open the
blade a mite, and most importantly, try to feel the left
hand holding the bade open as you come into the ball

A ball lower than the feet, will tend to slide right
as you well know. Allow for a slight fade, and stand an
inch or two nearer the ball. This should be a cup of tea
shot for you.

Finally under pressure --go with the shot which you have
the most confidence in. As you play with superior players
or your peers, you may be inclined to copy some of their
successful swings. Fine --if they work -- if not go back
to what you have. It takes more than a perfect swing to
make a champion, and because of musclatures, the best for
one, may not be the best for another.

Good Luck:

George

Pepper to play in LPGA event

CORNING — Dottie Pepper will be playing in the Ladies Professional Golf Association's Corning Classic later this month.

Pepper, a golf star at Saratoga High School, fired a 76 Monday in qualifying round action at the Corning Country Club to win a berth in the tournament.

Pepper, who will attend Furman in the fall, was second in the qualifier, finishing one stroke off the pace.

The Corning Classic will be held May 26-29.

Appeared in "Saratogian" May 17, 1983

Pepper Qualifies For LPGA Corning Classic

CORNING — Dottie Pepper, a senior at Saratoga High School, qualified for the Ladies Professional Golf Association Corning Classic yesterday, shooting a 76 in a qualifying round at the Corning Country Club.

Pepper, who will attend Furman University next year, was the second low qualifier, one stroke off the leader. The Corning Classic, which runs May 26-29, will be Pepper's first LPGA Tour...

Appeared in "Schenectady Gazette" May 17, 1983

Pepper to play in Corning golf

CORNING — Saratoga High senior Dottie Pepper will be in the starting field when the LPGA Corning Classic starts today at the Corning Country Club.

The 17-year-old Pepper will be one of three amateurs in the event as she shot a 76 in a qualifying round at Corning recently. More than 100 pros are entered in the 72-hole tournament, which has a purse of $150,000.

Pepper will tee off at 8:18 a.m. today with professionals Brenda Goldsmith of San Antonio, Tex., and Karen Permezel of Yackandandah, Australia.

"You know I'm really excited about this," Pepper said before heading to Corning. "I know I'm going to be a little nervous at the start, but I think if I can shoot a couple of 75s I can make the cut."

Pepper's second round will start at 12:54 p.m. Friday. The field will be cut to the low 70 and ties after 36 holes.

Appeared in "Times Union" May 26, 1983

Morse, Pepper in Golf Field

(Combined Dispatches)
CORNING — The Capital District will have two representatives in the field when the Ladies Professional Golf Association makes its annual tour stop here today for the $150,000 Corning Classic.

Cathy Morse, a six-year professional from Albany, will tee it up today, as will Dottie Pepper of Saratoga Springs, who will be competing as an amateur.

Morse has struggled somewhat this year after finishing 20th on the LPGA earnings list a year ago with over $70,000. Pepper, meanwhile, a former state amateur champion who is headed for Furman University in the fall on a golf scholarship, qualified for this tourney earlier in the month.

The largest field ever on the 6,286-yard, par 72 Corning Country Club course includes 105 professionals and three amateurs.

Sandra Spuzich, who became the oldest player ever to win an LPGA event here last year at age 45, now views the Corning Classic as a nest egg.

"I hope it's going to be the Sandra Spuzich Retirement Fund," she said this week while tuning up for the tournament, which runs through Sunday.

Spuzich, who shares the 72-hole record with Patty Sheehan at 280, was thinking only of the $22,500 first prize to carry her through the next century. Corning is the first step to the biggest purse ever offered LPGA regulars. The champion here will go on to West Virginia Classic in Wheeling next week and the July 14-17 McDonald's Classic in Malvern, Pa., with the chance of winning $1.35 million.

A golfer must win all three for the full prize, but two of three titles would merit $450,000.

Dave Goff, Corning tournament publicist, said the money was insured and would be paid over 10 years starting in 1993.

By then, Spuzich would be 56, but the 21-year veteran said she might still be around after making 1982 her best year on tour with two victories and $89,822 in winnings.

"It's a myth that people can't perform after age 40. If you keep yourself in good mental shape and stay in good condition, you can win at any age," she said.

The proof of that might be Hall of Famer JoAnne Carner, 44, drawn to Corning by the potential of the bonus triple. After four weeks off, Carner still ranks 10th in 1983 winnings with $69,969 in just eight events.

A 37-time champion and the LPGA player of the year twice in the last three years, Carner heads the list of LPGA millionaires with $1,418,913 in career money. Four of five other seven-figure winners — Kathy Whitworth, Donna Caponi, last week's champion Pat Bradley and Amy Alcott — also will play.

Alcott, 27, leads the money parade this year with $100,143, followed by Whitworth with $93,631.

Nancy Lopez, the only tour millionaire to skip the event, is third in 1983 winnings with $86,448, while Bradley and Beth Daniel rank fourth and fifth. Jan Stephenson, Alice Miller, Janet Coles and Hollis Stacy, who rank sixth through ninth, are not entered at Corning, but Carner and Sheehan hold the next two places with $69,969 and $62,192, respectively.

Appeared in "Schenectady Gazette" May 26, 1983

Dottie's news clippings from May 1983

The trip to the state high school championship was overall a positive one. I finished in the top third of the field as the only girl competing on a wet course tipped out at well over 7,000 yards. That was followed by a runner-up finish at the AJGA event at Stratton, but the longer look at the summer had the Gazette Women's Amateur coming up quickly, a tournament I dearly wanted to win after wicked defeats at the hands of Alice Baker the previous two years. Two state championships and the U.S. Girls Junior were on the schedule as well. Regarding the Gazette event, I simply had not checked the Pulver box of "defeating everyone within three hundred miles four out of five times." I hadn't even beaten Alice and the rest of the field once in the biggest women's amateur event in the Capital District!

Teachers and students are bound to have days when they're just a bit "off." July 2 was apparently one of those days. Knowing me, I was likely amped up about the Gazette tournament and not paying attention to the present. But leave it to the well-read Mr. Pulver to bring Sophocles into the post-lesson wrap-up. Mr. Pulver felt he talked too much, and I was clearly not in good form either.

July, 2, 1983
MISS DOTTIE PEPPER:

GJP

DOTTIE:

A wise old Greek by the name of Sophocles is supposed to have said: "Much wisdom often goes with the fewest words." Today, I think that I talked too much. Emotions, whatever, your timing today was a little ragged -- very little else. I urge you to work on the following:

In any practice, or warm-ups prior to playing, please start with the #5 iron, after you have hit a few wedges. Using but 80% of you power, try to start back slowly, and especially start down from the top in the same leisurely manner. When the #5 irons feel solid, reach for the Driver and with no more power effort, try to capture the same feeling as you did with the #5 iron. God, alone, knows how difficult this is to do.

Consensus would probably agree, the two most dritical parts of the golf swing to be the start-back, and even more importantly the start-down Yes, we have had great champions, like Hogan Lanny Watkins, and presently Watson, who go back and down with lightning rapidity. but toe most players, a slower up and staart-down is wiser.

You have a magnificent Upright-Swing--by the way the swing of the fluture. Lets work on your rythm. Your mechanics are already superlative!

See you around, and good luck.

George,

We always had a straightforward, comfortable way of talking to each other, keeping our concerns and thoughts out in the open. He never saw my questions as silly; he never passed judgment. He always ended a letter with a positive comment. Here, he added a simple directive about working on my rhythm.

I did get that big win in the Gazette a week later and while to many it may have seemed to be "just a local tournament," to me it was an enormous step, not only because I had given up leads to lose in some of those previous tournaments but because it reinforced my stature as someone who could win at every level. I believe this is crucial in junior development. I see kids being shipped off to academies and entered into national tournaments when they can't even beat everyone in their own area code.

Another related thought: It's OK to win and to win by big margins at every level. Learn to keep your foot on the gas and reset personal scoring goals when things are going great and leads are being stretched. It's not often we find ourselves cruising in the thin air of near-perfection. Hammer it when it happens and enjoy every second.

By this time, I was looking for more distance by adding a lighter, graphite shafted driver. I'd been watching the longer players and that seemed to be a missing piece of the puzzle. The quest for distance is certainly not a new topic, as nearly 40 years later the subject of distance has consumed nearly every conversation in and around golf. My search had hit home with Mr. Pulver, quite literally as he wrote this to his son, George, Jr. Money was tight and a new driver just wasn't happening.

Mr. Pulver quickly switched back to George, Jr.'s game. Young George, a wonderful player in his own right, was now in his mid-40s and his dad was clearly thinking he needed to refine his equipment choices. It's always nice when your parents remind you of your advancing age! He also dropped in a not-so-subtle reminder to his grandson ("that boy of yours") about his own swing being too upright and trying to hit the ball too hard. Once a teacher, always a teacher.

I discovered this letter to George much later in the process of writing this book and what struck me not only was Mr. Pulver's unwavering belief in my abilities and future but also that I had been looped right in with his own kids and grandkids. I was just one of them. There was the teacher-student relationship but there was also a grandfatherly role he filled as well.

Wednesda y, July 3rd:

George:

Recently, Dottie wrote me about graphyte shafts, saying that she needed more distance. Please return my copy at once. The club cost $150.00 -- the Father said no way.

Now I would like to return to graphyte --

The next time you come to Saratoga, bring your old stiff shafted Driver, and your new bbig club. I want to check them. You are getting older, and it may well be that the original stiff shafted driver would be lighter and enhance your hand speed. Remember, I would like to compare your new big Driver, with the stiff shafted graphyte you use to use.

George --Dottie may not win tomorrow, or soon, but she shall most surely win big o e of these days. Get that boy of yours to go back in one piece, around his body, before he elevates the club out of plane with his hands, his swing is too upright, and he is trying to hit the ball too hard.

Say hello to all the family and hang in there. !

Dad:

George Pulver, Jr., at the Saratoga Golf Club

I distinctly remember the anxiety Mr. Pulver's next letter brought to our house. I was quickly getting stronger and I needed equipment to match. But there just wasn't the money to make it happen.

July 10, 1983

DOTTIE:

Should your father and mother agree -- I recommend the purchase of a second driver. You would then have two driving clubs at Furman. The older one with a much softened shaft, and a newer one slightly firmer that could better match your growing vigor and power.

Your swing is superlative. However, from time to time, slowly encourage the adoption of a two knuckle grip with your left hand, rather than your present three knuckle one.

Finally, I feel that a slightly firmer shaft shall improve your driving accuracy, perhaps not your length.

See your around.

P. S. Attach, specifications of new driver, which the artisans at the factory will clearly understand.

zip 12831

Specifications: Miss Dottie Pepper, Box 196, Worth Road, Gansevoort, N. Y.

Driver 43 inchhes long,
Swing weight about D
Grip Rubber, Ladies Oversized, Brown
Shaft, Firm A, one-half inch tipped
Head, current stratablock, as used by advanced players.

Ultimately I did get that new driving club just before leaving for college in early September. Jack Conger, the head professional at Pompey Hills (where I lost in the final of the state junior the year before) had become a family friend and, hearing of the dilemma, graciously provided the MacGregor Eye-O-Matic persimmon driver at wholesale. It was absolutely gorgeous and perfectly fit for me.

My parents were, of course, extremely appreciative of Mr. Pulver's help and guidance, but it is his response to a thank you note from them that shows how timely the beginning of our relationship was for his life after Mrs. Pulver. Our relationship certainly proved timely and helpful for me, but perhaps more important, it offered a positive path and focus for him. George and Martha were inseparable, and her loss left an enormous void in every part of his life.

Mr. Pulver,

So much time has passed since we last expressed our appreciation for your time and effort helping Dottie achieve her goals. You are a large part of it. With deep respect and gratitude we thank-you for the lessons and wisdom you share with her.

Our Sincere thanks,

Lynn & Don Pepper

July 22, 1983

Jul 24, 1983

Don & Mrs Pepper
Worth Road,
Saratoga Springs, N. Y.

First of all, let me hasten to thank you for that class shirt. Dottie delivered to me on Friday. More importantly, the color and fit are perfect.

Please understand, when I first saw Dottie swing, I knew as a golf teacher, she had pure talent. It was not a particular happy moment for me because of the loss of Martha, but Dottie's swing and grace galvanized my attention. Her progress is my reward.

It is my only hope, that in some small way, I can nudge her along in her burning desire to be a fine golfer. She shall win some -- she shall most surely lose some. She should not get too crestfallen when she fails. The way to the top is a zig-zag course. Her swing has beauty, power, and is modern. But most importanly, is her determination, her mind, and her heart.

Sincerely,

George J. Pulver,

We had worked hard over two years to refine my technique but, again, what mattered most to him was determination, mind, and heart. Beautiful golf swings without those three factors are just that — beautiful golf swings.

The win at the state junior girls event was also a big one, not only because of the loss in the previous year's final but because of age restrictions; it would be the last time I was eligible to play in the tournament. I also got the chance to win and win big — and took it with an 8 & 7 victory over Jennifer Dunster.

Dottie with the cup following her win at the New York State Junior Girls Championship
Photo credit: Betty Deeley

Betty Deeley organized and ran the girls' and women's championships in New York, and we had become very close over the previous three years. Winning that final junior championship at her home course, McConnellsville C.C., made the win even more special — for her and for me. She traveled to see me play professional golf when my

Dottie and Betty Deeley. Photo courtesy of the NYSGA

career got to that point. She even sat with me in a TV booth or two when I moved to that part of my career. Golf in New York State would look very different if it wasn't for the love and dedication of Betty Deeley, whose young championship participants were known simply as "Betty's Girls." Mrs. Deeley would become part of the inaugural class of the New York State Golf Hall of Fame in 2012.

My introduction to USGA championships and the course in Bernardsville, New Jersey, designed by architect A.W. Tillinghast would be up next. I still remember being a bit awed by the experience of simply checking in at player registration at Somerset Hills C.C., signing the player scroll and playing a course of that stature for the first time.

The second-hole "redan" at Somerset Hills. Photo courtesy of Somerset Hills C.C.

Standing on the second tee and seeing a redan-style hole for the first time made me think, "What the heck am I going to do with this hole?" Mr. Pulver and I had talked about architecture and how to play different holes on many different courses, but this was golf in a much bigger theater than what I was used to. I had played so much golf at McGregor and learned to play the shots required to get around the well-respected Devereaux Emmet design, but this was another beast all together. And I loved it! The experience at Somerset Hills certainly triggered a curiosity and appreciation about golf course architecture that I still have today.

It was more of that "Little Engine That Could" mentality that got me easily into match play. I beat a highly touted Susie Pager 6&4 in round three and figured I was on my way. But then I suffered a thorough thumping by Buffy Klein in the quarterfinals.

Lesson learned: Don't start writing your winner's speech until your hands are firmly on the trophy.

Mr. Pulver's response to the week was as expected. I was definitely down after hoping to go to Furman with a national championship on my resume. But he shed a lot of perspective when he mentioned the great Jack Nicklaus' 19 runner-up finishes in majors. Mr. Pulver's belief of looking at today's losses to build for tomorrow's successes was clear and consistent.

August 13, 1983

MISS DOTTIE PEPPER:

DOTTIE:

Welcome Back.-- You accomplished much! This was no city, county, or even State event, You were matching shots with 150 of the most promising girl golfers from this broad land. You toiled in enervating heat, on a strange course.

Always, success in Golf, is a zig-zag thing. Even the great Nichlaus has suffered 19 important and critical defeats, in his long illustrious career. Your losses today, are the payments you must make, in order to clutch the wins of tomorrow. Be patient, and look down the road.

It will be nice to see you at the range, at your inclination.

GP:
Geo

"Always, success in golf is a zig-zag thing. Even the great (Nicklaus) has suffered 19 important and critical defeats." — George Pulver

Another big thing for Mr. Pulver was always staying the course, never making any big, wholesale changes. He most certainly operated under the "if it ain't broke, don't fix it" philosophy.

Making a grip change can be big and uncomfortable for anyone, but he simplified that daunting task by asking me to change my strong left-hand grip to one that was a bit more neutral, with markers along the way so I could gauge my own progress. He was always striving to make me more self-reliant and able to diagnose my own problems.

In this letter, note again how he continually hammered home the importance of the unhurried takeaway and its direction. He was absolutely relentless in making sure I knew the importance of this basic building block to a repeatable swing.

Being a cautious man, Mr. Pulver also made sure I was aware of the downsides and distractions of other forces in and around amateur and professional sports, keeping up his practice of clipping and sending articles from a wide variety of sources. Steroid use and a trendy overemphasis on sports psychology were particularly worrisome for him.

August 21, 1983

MISS DOTTIE PEPPER:

DOTTIE:

Your swing looks good to me. Any aberation, no doubt to be the result of too early release of right hand, brought on by pressure.

However, little by little, I would urge about a two knuckle grip with the left hand, as you look down. The thumb, should rest along side of shaft, not on top. On top would block out too much. If the V of the left hand points at the shoulder(right), the right hand will usually adjust.

Notwithstanding, I do feel a light weight steel shaft (R) would help. It is more forgiving. Of course choose the head and make you prefer. In the meanwhile take the club slowly straight back, and try to guide the club down with the left hand and arm, slightly inside of the path taken on the way back. This is a rather fleeting thing, but you can do it with peripheral vision. Your turn and your lower body is ex-cellent.

August 31, 1983

MISS DOTTIE PEPPER:

DOTTIE:

Enclosed, a recent article from the magazine section of the Sunday
Times. I must warn you that such articles are too much for my simple
peasant mind. Stearoids, and now Sports Pschology, may be making a
lot of zombies out of our very young. The lines underscored in red,
I cana probably go along with.

In virtually all endeavors, those who succeed work harder, think deeper,
and continue in their undiminished zeal towards definite goals. Often,
chance darts at them, for the good or bad. Surely, a promising future
lies before you.

George

Just two paragraphs in length, this letter — the last he would write before I left for
my freshman year at Furman — sums up the grit and grace necessary for success in
any sport. It helps manage the often overwhelming feeling of needing to keep up with
every hot trend: "In virtually all endeavors, those who succeed work harder, think
deeper and continue in their undiminished zeal toward definite goals," he wrote. Set
your goals, both short- and long-term, and refuse to be deterred. You will have speed
bumps but never lose sight of what you love and are trying to achieve.

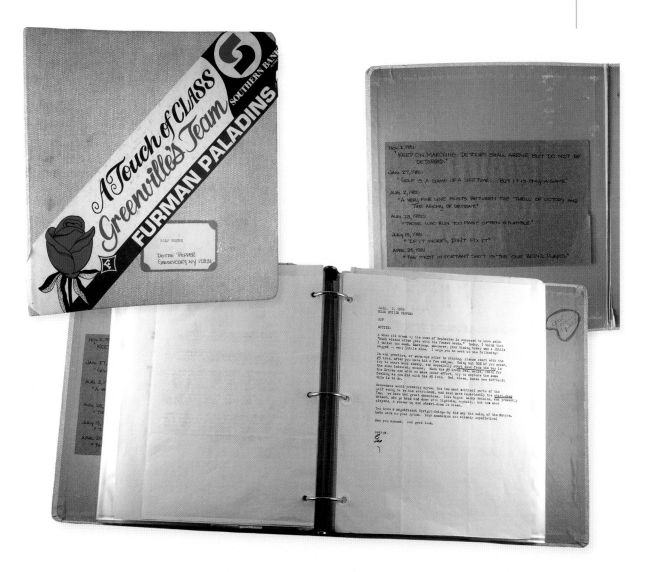

Our relationship would transition to a long-distance, even more letter-intensive one as I made my way to college and would not return home until Christmas. One thing I made sure I packed was my three-ring binder of Mr. Pulver's letters and the page outline from the Snead book. This was mandatory. The original letters are still in that binder today.

I didn't have the money for many long distance calls to Mr. Pulver, but I had a lot of 20-cent stamps, and I simply enjoyed writing to him, sharing the ups and downs of college life, the adjustments both in the classroom and on the golf course, just playing in college competitions for the first time. I was always so happy to find a letter from him in my post office box in the student center, often reading it before I got out of the building. There were even times I took the notebook itself to practice for easy reference.

Sept. 7, 1988

Dear Mr. Pulver,

Hi! I'm at school now and things are going well. I've played 27 holes since being down here and I'm playing pretty well. Our qualifying starts on next Friday. We play 18 holes on Friday, 18 on Saturday and 36 on Sunday. On the 23rd we leave for Florida State and on the 30th we leave for Memphis State. Both of them are 54 hole tournaments. I'm really looking forward to the tournaments. Tuesday we got our new team golf bags. They're great. Today we get our new clothes: shorts, shirts, sweaters, gore-tex rain gear plus a new umbrella. We're going to have a really strong team this year. We may even have a shot at the NCAA title.

As far as school goes, we're still in the orientation part of the year. This afternoon I have to take a placement test in Spanish at 1:00. Classes begin on Tuesday, the 13th. I think I'm going to take Math, English, and Religion this semester.

Yesterday I got my new address and telephone number. Here it is:

Dottie Pepper
P.O. Box 27934
Furman University
Greenville, South Carolina 29613.

Telephone: (803) 294-2428

Mom and Dad are still down here. They'll be going home early Friday morning. It was a very nice trip down here but Virginia, Pennsylvania and North Carolina are extremely dry. Many cities like Charlotte, N.C. are on a water alert.

Well- I'm running out of room so I'll say good-bye for now. I'll be looking forward to hearing from you. Take care.

Love-
Dottie

I also knew he and Martha had three children who went to undergrad schools and beyond; there was nothing I could tell him about college pressures that he would not have already been through with Jean, Madelyn, and George Jr. He placed an enormous emphasis on education, and I wanted to check that box on his list of "must do's" as well.

Mr. George Pulver, Sr.
136 East Avenue
Saratoga Springs, N.Y. 12866

September 15, 1983

MISS DOTTIE PEPPER
P. O. Box 27934
Furman University
Greenville, S. C. 29613

DOTTIE:

I am always interested and happy to hear from you.

It was sustaining, that your Father and Mother, were able to
go South with you. Going alone to a new and challenging environment,
indeed one can use the support of her entire family.

Your team must present a formidable and attractive group, embellished
with your shining new gear.

You show great wisdom in your majors. In the life which lies before us,
only the good Lord knows how much we all need Faith, English, and Math.

YOUR SWING -- It is better than good, as I have often remarked. You
should make no major swing changes unless forced to. Should your shots
start to wander -- look to your timing. Bunt out balls, swinging a slow easy
$5 iron. Then switch to your big wood.

The hard part, make an effort to start down with the same cadence you started
back with --SLOWLY. This also applies to putting on fast greens.

It is certain from time to time, that tensions and other anxieties shall
surely surface. And the mental side--concentrate on the shot being played,
and not on the ones which have passed, or lie ahead. I wish I could do
these things. You can*!

If you feel that I can be of any help from time to time, write me.

Geo

Making the transition to Furman Golf Club's common Bermuda surfaces was a major challenge and one that didn't come easily for someone who played nearly all of her golf on northern poa annua or bent grass.

Sept. 30

Dear Mr. Pulver,

Hi. How are you doing? I hope all is going fine for you. I'm adjusting to college life pretty well. My studies are extremely difficult but I'm managing to get by O.K. My golf is improving. Now that I've got my first college tournament under my belt, I feel alot better. Last week (Sept. 25-27) we played in the Florida State Lady Seminole Invitational. I shot 76-76-79. I should have played much better that last day but I just couldn't get the ball in the hole. I'm swining great and I've got alot more confidence in my ball striking ability. I'm hitting more fairways and greens than I ever have before. Yesterday we had qualifying for the Memphis State tournament. I shot 74 and came in first. I had it even par through 16 holes with 14 pars, and birdie and a bogey but I double bogeyed the 17th and parred the final hole. Oh well. We are leaving for the tournament this afternoon at 1:00. It is going to be a 10 hour drive to Memphis. The tournament begins on the 2nd and runs through the 4th. We are the defending champions there. I should play really well because we are going to be playing on bent grass there. I'll just have to spend a little time on my short game adjusting it to the bent grass again. I'm really getting to like the Bermuda grass, though. We have really good Bermuda at our course at school. The Bermuda at Florida State wasn't that good. The greens and tees had a lot of native grasses in them.

The weather has been very good here ever since I've been here. Usually it is in the mid to lower 80s and pretty sunny. We haven't had much humidity at all considering this is South Carolina. We have had a couple of really could mornings but I can't complain. I understand it has been quite cold up there.

Well, I have to be going to my next class and then I have to get re: to leave so I will say good-bye for now. I will look forward to hearing from you. Miss you, alot! Love - Dottie

It also was not easy to have essentially entered college on academic probation, because while my high school grades were really good, my SAT scores were pathetic. If I flunked out, I knew my parents couldn't afford to keep me in a private school; I'd be coming home and going to a local community college.

On top of the academic pressure, Furman also had a no-exceptions freshman attendance policy that would mean missing one of the tournaments on our fall schedule. There were times when I felt like I was drowning in pressure and expectation. Learning how to study in college, where and when to study, how to balance long hours of travel in the team van, practice, qualifying, and tournament play, just living on my own for the first time, dorm life, never having been on a women's team before — all of it was borderline-overwhelming. But sharing it with Mr. Pulver was both a release and a gift.

Mr. Pulver continued to send clippings along with his letters, this time showing favor with Amy Alcott and her strong will and determination. He also shared a gem in closing that is absolutely evergreen: "Continue to the very last shot. Success may dart at you at any moment."

```
MISS DOTTIE PEPPER:
October 5, 1983
DOTTIE:

Your letter of Sept. 30, cataloguing your efforts thus far as Furmond,
indeed captures my interest.

Away from home for perhaps for the first time, Freshmen find their first
year at once bewildering and trying.  I learned from my children who all
went down that road.  New surroundings, new friends, and work.  However,
I predict your following years shall be less demanding.

Being on a golf scholarship, many hours of driving range labors lie before
you.  However, as you remarked, about four months during the Winter months,
you may find time time to take a more thorough peep at your books.  Obvioussly,
your golf must come first.

Your mention of Bermuda.  Personally, I have always preferred Bermuda to
Bent to putt on.  It seems Bermuda blades to be more perpendicular, that
the low lying deceptive Bents.  But, of course, you must learn both grasses.

Dottie, from time to time, I may feel the urge to include some clippings.
Note the enclosed by Amy Olcott.  Certainly, her philosopy  her hardness,
her desire to overcome,  must have been stronger tools, than her swing.

You shall be constantly learning from your successes as well as your failures.
Certain courses and terrains may embrace your game -- others shall most certain-
ly reject your best efforts. Continue to the very last shot.  Sucess may dart
at you at any moment.

George:
```

When people ask about closing out tournaments, this quote comes to mind because we cannot control our opponents and their performance. What we can always do is play through the finish, not to the finish. Great thoroughbreds don't run to the finish line, they run through it. Great golfers don't play to the 18th, they play through it, too.

My fall-term freshman-year golf really wasn't very good. A tie for 22nd in the first event was the best I could do. However, Mr. Pulver's letters certainly put things in perspective and always provided both pops of confidence and a reminder that this was all part of a larger learning process. I was definitely not getting straight A's in the patience department, but he also knew the Type A personality he was dealing with.

When I was finally home for Christmas, it was so good to share the experiences of the first term at school with Mr. Pulver, sitting in the living room of his humble home on East Avenue. This summation letter was one of the longest he wrote, but it included a much-needed checklist of the fundamentals he preached, a caution about over-thinking and seeing the experiences of the past four months though his own filters.

He was spot-on in saying that this could well be the toughest year for adjustments. It was indeed. But as hard as it was, I still believe kids need to go to college, if only to experience those highs and lows. They're better for having a go at it on their own, learning how to manage a college budget, balancing sports and academics, surviving on short sleep, setting priorities, making mistakes, and living with roommates and teammates you don't always adore.

The year had begun with an aggressive list of events and goals, most of which I had good showings in, and more of the "Pulver boxes" were checked. I managed to do well enough at school to be out of the academic woods and play in every tournament I was eligible. Pretty solid overall. But, of course, I was looking for much more.

October 25, 1983

MISS DOTTIE PEPPER,
P. O. Box 27934
Furman University,
Greensville, S. C. 29613

Dottie:

Inre your letter of October 21st:

Always its exams of some kind. But abide -- they are the requisites of direction and mental enlargement. Golf, you shall find, shall be up and down. Again, try not to make many swing changes, but persevere, and you shall be a credit to your family, and your home area.

I still feel very strongly, about beating balls on a range. Its the only way to sort out the chaff, from the wheat. Try to learn to discern, why some shots are perfect, and others go awry. Of course, along the way, pick up pointers from your peers, as I am sure they shall filch from your swing.

Your mention, of some goodies left at my house by your mother. This reminds me I have not acknowledge her goodies, but shall correct this ommission at once.

I never really knew your grandmother, but there is one thing I do know. She is a happy person to be around and know. You shall be lonely at times, being your first year away from home, Your grandmother is the right kind of tonic. Then later you may see your father, and often you receive packages from your Mother. We all can use some family strength, and we need it constantly. Always, I have found your mother a person of rare spirit, and intellect.

Madelyn, has been out on the West Coast for the past three weeks, but this week-end, she may be back in Saratoga. George and Jean are well, and your interest is indeed appreciated.

This past week, the erie cries of the Geese heading South, high in the heavens, is an ominous omen, of that which shall soon follow. Hit the ball when you can, and hit the books when you are least urged to, do so. I attach a clipping of Raymond Floyd. His words make enormous sense to an aspiring minded golfer. I am always please to learn of your health and game, but only at your leisure.

George J. Pulver, Sr.,

P. S.) That new Driver must be working --perhaps not longer, but surely more constant response.

George Pulver watches closely as daughter Madelyn practices her iron play.

"I feel very strongly, about beating balls on a range. It's the only way to sort out the chaff, from the wheat. Try to learn to discern, why some shots are perfect, and others go awry." — *George Pulver*

TOURNAMENT RECORD

1983 - (Age 17-18)

- Qualified but missed cut, LPGA Corning Classic, Corning C.C.

- T-30 New York State Boys High School Championship, Cornell University Golf Club (only girl in field)

- Runner-up, AJGA Northern Junior, Stratton Mountain G.C.

- Winner, Gazette Women's Amateur Championship, Willows C.C.

- Lost in semifinals, New York State Women's Amateur Championship, Seven Oaks G.C.

- Winner, New York State Junior Girls Championship, McConnellsville C.C.

- Lost in quarterfinals, USGA Junior Girls Championship, Somerset Hills C.C.

- T-22, Florida State Lady Seminole Invitational, Florida State University Golf Club

- T-25, Memphis State Carrier Classic, Stonebridge C.C.

- T-32, Pat Bradley Invitational, Crandon Golf at Key Biscayne

- T-38 Suncoast Invitational, Innisbrook Resort (Island Course)

The start of my college golf career hadn't exactly been the start I had envisioned, and shortly after Christmas, Dad was involved in a serious car accident, one that required a fairly lengthy hospitalization and his right shoulder to be almost entirely rebuilt. Life seemed really tumultuous and filled with a lot of anxiety, both family-wise and golf-wise after my mediocre fall results.

1/4/84

Dear Mr. Pilver —

I'm sorry I didn't get a chance to say good-bye to you before I left for school yesterday. With Dad's car accident and surgery last week, the latter part of my vacation was, to say the least, a complete shambles. But I suppose we just have to accept life's bumps and jolts as we go along. It seems good to be back at school with all of my friends. Being warm and being able to play golf again is terrific, but I miss home alot. In fact, I think I miss home more now than when I left in September. I'm taking English, First Aid, and Physical Education this term. This winter term is a compacted term: 13 weeks worth of work is crammed into 8 weeks. The term ends February 25. This afternoon I talked to our coach about going home for the vacation that starts on the 25th and he said I shouldn't go home. Since I am so close to Atlanta, do you think Jean would mind me staying with her from then until March 4th? Getting transportation to Atlanta would be no problem. All I would need is a place to lie my head at night and a place to hit some golf balls. I would really appreciate it if you would mention it to her since I'll need to make other arrangements if this don't work out. I don't want her to go out of her way for this and I don't want ~~anyone~~ to make any inconvenience for her. Going back north for a week and then going to the University of Texas the following week just isn't conducive to good golf.

We're expected to have a warm winter here in the Carolinas — I only hope the Farmer's Almanac is right. Christmas certainly was cold up home. Today was a sunny 60° and was so comfortable. I hope spring comes early up in New York — I know how much you dislike being indoors all the time.

I will keep in touch with you until I'm northward bound again — then we can resume our ~~~~ practice and learning again. It certainly was wonderful spending some time with you during the past weeks.

Hope to hear from you soon.
Best Wishes for a terrific 1984 —
Love,
Dottie

P.S. Could you please send me Jean's address? Thank you. ☺

Going back to a condensed winter term was not going to be easy, but the good news was that space had opened in classes in my major, giving me a feeling like I was working more toward my actual degree in Sports Management, rather than solely toiling away at the gut, required courses every freshman trudges through.

With a short winter term and no tournament on my schedule for spring break, the big question was where to go before the golf team resumed play. I ended up grabbing a ride with a classmate south to my paternal grandmother's winter home in Melbourne, Florida, where I could beat balls and play the entire time.

Unfortunately, as so many young players do when they try to carve their own space in the game, I had gotten sucked into looking at too much video, getting too technical, taking on far too much advice, and trying to be too perfect. And it was far from perfect! It was more like ugly.

I had relied on Mr. Pulver's basics to get me to this point and then semi-ditched it all in an effort to improve. Somehow the word *refine* had been removed from my brain and instead replaced with *redo*. This is an all-too-common story; it is so important to get back to what you know works and polish that, not dispose of it. I've found that improvement in whatever you are doing is best thought of as a wide bell curve where there is a positive and satisfying zone of good. Not a steep, narrow curve with a quick ascent of learning, a sharp, fleeting point of perfection, then painful decline in performance on the other side. Better to have a more steady trajectory of improvement over time, eventually resulting in consistent excellence.

I wrote to Mr. Pulver (see next page) confessing my backsliding but assured him I was back to focusing on his way rather than the "help" from others.

I sarcastically referred to worrying about what my eyebrows were doing (yep, overthinking the whole thing) and that, truthfully, golf was becoming fun again. Mr. Pulver must have been shaking his head reading this mess and muttering, "I tried to tell her." It is important, however, that I made my own mistakes and learned from them. That part of the process he most assuredly enjoyed.

February and March were always the time to start putting the summer tournament schedule together and setting goals for those events. I would have one last shot at a junior title because of the AJGA's age policy (18 years old was their maximum), but it would also be another summer of the best tournaments in the women's game, both amateur and professional, coming to the Northeast. Among those events was the U.S. Women's Open at Salem C.C. in Peabody, Massachusetts, and the Women's Western Amateur in New Haven, Connecticut. The same economics still applied: If you can drive, you can play. Checking that "Pulver box" for consistent wins in the 300-mile circle around Saratoga Springs was still very much part of the planning.

2-26-84

Dear Mr. Pulver—

Hi! Sorry it has been so long since I've written, but now that I'm on my spring break I've got a chance to write all of my over-due letters. Everything has been going well for me lately. The winter term at school went great. I even have a chance of making the Dean's list.

I'm at my grandmother's in Florida right now. The weather has been wonderful at school, but it's even better here. I'll be here until next Sunday so I'll have lots of time to get rested and work on my game. Our winter qualifying tournament at school went great and I made my 15 state. My scores were really consistent: 73–76. I played very well today and shot 67. Next Wednesday we're leaving for our first spring tournament. It's at the University of Texas. I'm really looking forward to this spring and summer.

I've decided that my "old" swing is best and have ignored the "help" from our coach this winter. I'm much happier and confident not having to worry about what my eyebrows are doing all the time!! I keep reading the letters that you've sent me and that solves all the little problems like timing or alignment or anything else. Golf is actually fun now — this fall it was awful! I've planned out my schedule for this summer. I want to be selected to the Curtis Cup team next year, so the schedule is geared toward selection to the team. All the tournaments fall in June and July but once they're over, I'll be able to relax at the start for awhile, play some fun golf and work on my game so I'll be ready for our

The biggest summer prize would be a spot on the Curtis Cup Team, the biennial women's amateur competition between the United States team and the team from Great Britain and Ireland. I knew I would probably have to win out in the spring schedule to have any shot at selection, but you may as well aim high — and also keep in mind that accumulating great finishes wouldn't hurt a bid for the 1986 team either.

Mr. Pulver's response in early March covered many subjects. It struck high notes on the importance of reinforcing what you already do well, sticking to your go-to shot unless another is required, academics ("Keep thinking!"), becoming more comfortable on Bermuda grass, concentration, and always reminding me to "Hang In There." It's impossible not to notice his closing thought, however. He loved the fact that

school schedule to start in September. I'm very fortunate that so many great tournaments are in the northeast this year.

This term at school I'm taking Geology, History, and Sports Sociology. It will be hard because of all our tournaments, but I'll make it. I'll be out of school on May 30th and will be home on June 2nd. I'm really looking forward to our lessons again.

Dad's arm is getting better quickly — he may even be playing golf when the season starts again at home. The operation was a total success as far as the doctors can tell at this point. He's gaining mobility and strength in it everyday.

I hope everything is going well for you. Spring isn't far away and you'll be at the course again soon!

Take care — I'll see you in a few short months.

Miss you a lot.

Love,
Dottie

I wasn't travel-weary in finding the best competition, much of which was in the Northeast again.

Mr. Pulver was never satisfied in his pursuit of golf knowledge and he worked at his trade tirelessly, whether by reading, watching, playing, or sharing thoughts with other professionals. It was a constant search for what makes a better game and what makes a champion.

March 3, 1984

Miss Dottie Pepper
P. O. Box 27934
Furman University,
Greenville, S. C. 29619

DOTTIE:

I was indeed delighted to get your recent letter of February 26th.
Your catalogue of your efforts and progress interested me.

First to golf: In my humble view, your natural manner of attacking
a golf ball is an excellent one, and has already hardened into a very
effective method. And by the way, brought you abundant accolades.
Work to improve that which already you do so well.

All your power shots, set up about square, with your shoulders, hips,
and knees -- your stance slightly closed, to promote bringing the ball
in from right to left. However, since Nichlaus and his successes with
a fade, too many courses are designed to move the ball from left to right.
This should be a cup of tee for you, but we shall take a look at such a
flight only when it is required.

Your academic achievements, no less than your golf schedule, are superior
in every way. Keep thinking! I still feel the first year to be the most
enervating, to a young college student, far from home, in a strange land.

Glad to learn that your Father is doing well with his injury. He is a
strong individual, possessing impeccable physiological assets.

Yes, your mention of the warmth and charm of Florida, arouses a nostalgia
to return, since I spent more than twenty winters there. But not really!
Without Martha by my side, I fear the anticipated would be but a mirarge.

It was super that you got to Florida, to visit with your strong and happy
Grandmother. and at the same time to further your knowledge of Bermuda,
and tropical courses.

Finally, work as much as you can on concentration. In actual play, to
the very end try to do your best. Some days it will not work, but don't
dispair, Hang in There!.

I COMMEND YOU ON YOUR SUMMER GOLF SCHEDULE, AND SO MUCH IN THE NORTHEAST.

With every good wish

George J. Pulver.

Dattis

March 20, 1984

The first time that I saw a great golfer play, was in 1913, at the
Equinox club at Marnchester, Vermont. He was the immortal Vardon,
playing Ted Ray. in an exhibition. At that time I was a caddie at
the Saratoga Golf Club, and one of its members, J. K. Walbridge,
invited me to ride with him to Manchester.

Vardon, was actually not a big men, perhaps 5' 9''. He stood slightly
open to his flight line, and playeda fade on virtually all of his shots.
Oh Yes! At the top, he bent his left arm a great deal.

The next world class golfer that I saw play , was the great Hagen. His
swing was sort of bravado -- using a rolling head in going back and coming
through, and he too bent his left arm at the top. I took pictures of his
swing --he appeared to be playing all right handed. HE WAS SOME GOLFER'.

A number of years later, I went out to the middle of the State, to witness
Trevino play an exhibition. As Trevino, came to the tee laughing and chattering,
one of the by-standers said to him --"You can never be a champion -- you lack
length. Trevino, pointed to a fairway bunker far down the fairway, and remarked how far is that trap? The bystander said 260 yards. Trevino, took
his Driver from his bag, and hit the bunker on the fly. I could not belive
my eyes. He stood Open to the ball, and looked like a man beating a pig.
BUT HE TOO, could play'.

In 1923, I was assistant golf professional at the Lake Placid Golf Club.
Glenna Collett was giving an exhibition, and for the very first time,
I saw the leading women golfer attack a golf ball, and she average about
200 yards off each tee, with hickory shafts, and the less resilient ball
of that era.

It must have been about 1960, and I took a trip to Fla. A pro-ladies tournament
was being played at St. Petersburg. One of my cracker friends introduced me
to JUDY RANKIN, and asked me to comment on her swing. I never though she would
get anywhere. She was slight, had he flattest swing I had ever seen, and her
grip was simply awful.

All of the players which I have named were unorthodox, except perheps, Glenna
Collett, and even she swayed and slugged at the ball. But before you conclude
I am making a case for the unorthodox player, I hasten to add, "The certainty
of a good sound swing will generally prevail.

But the case I do want to make, is that a sound swing is not·enough today.
One must have the undieing desire to get the ball into the hole and keep trying to the very end. This may be the magical difference between a fine player
and a champion. THINK!
→ THIS WAS AND IS OUR JUDY RANKIN.

Please no reply. I look forward to seeing you when you return. Please say
hello to your Father and Mother.

George:

Geo

This letter lists those observations over about a 60-year span, from 1913 in Manchester, Vermont, watching Harry Vardon play Ted Ray in an exhibition, to Glenna Collett (Vare) at Lake Placid, New York, to Lee Trevino playing an exhibition in central New York sometime in the 1970s.

He loved to point out how each may have had less-than-perfect swings or, in the case of Judy Rankin, her grip, but all possessed the undying will to get the ball in the hole faster than their opponents.

For me, Judy Rankin has been my George Pulver in the world of golf broadcasting: a mentor, a confidante, a critic but always a model for how to share one's knowledge of the game without making it about the person holding the microphone.

Lee Trevino at the 1971 U.S. Open. Photo by PGA of America via Getty Images.

Judy was voted into the World Golf Hall of Fame in 2000 and at the celebration held for her in Rancho Mirage, California, I was asked to say a few words about her, my two-time Solheim Cup captain. Among my comments were lines read directly from

Judy Rankin. Photo courtesy of Elizabeth Opalenik

Phil Mickelson and Judy Rankin. Photo courtesy of Judy Rankin.

Mr. Pulver's observations after watching her play around 1960 in St. Petersburg, Florida. As usual, his assessment was straight on: "I never thought she would get anywhere. She was slight, had the flattest swing I had ever seen, and her grip was simply awful."

My notations from the speech are on that letter and she was, indeed, the perfect combination of what he knew champions were made of: a swing that repeats for you and the will to fight through the end.

I had an opportunity to sit down with Judy Rankin while writing this book, a wide-ranging Zoom recording that could easily be a book itself. Her story is one that needs to be told but she, being extraordinarily humble and even at times a bit meek, would never do it herself. So, I will do it for her!

To set the stage, a bit of her personal history: Judy Torluemke was born in St. Louis on Feb. 18, 1945, to a family of very modest means. Golf found her, as she says, when her father took the family to a lighted driving range near home when she was just 6 years old. Her dad let her hit the ball, and she could really hit it!

Her mom would soon pass from brain cancer, but she continued to play small tournaments around St. Louis until her father — Judy still doesn't know quite how this happened — entered her in the National PeeWee in Orlando, Florida, as an 8-year-old. But instead of entering her in her age group, he entered her in the next group up.

With no money for travel, folks from a local nine-hole course gave her a new suitcase with $400 cash in it and off they went to Orlando in their old Nash Rambler. Judy would not only win that first National PeeWee but also win the event for the next three straight years. That strong left-hand grip that Mr. Pulver talked about took her all the way to the 1960 U.S. Women's Open at Worcester, Massachusetts, as a 15-year-old, where she became, at the time, the youngest low amateur in the history of that championship.

Snubbed by the USGA for a spot on the following summer's Curtis Cup team, Judy turned professional at age 16, playing nine LPGA events that year with a stipend of $150 a week from an endorsement deal with the First Flight company. She appeared on the cover of Sports Illustrated on Aug. 21, 1961. The cover's text: "The Best Girl Golfer." Talk about pressure on a youngster!

Judy would spend the next year not playing regularly on tour but rather at a club in Philadelphia, working in the golf shop, playing late in the day, honing her skills and often playing with another assistant professional there, Bert Yancey. Yancey would go on to win seven times on the PGA Tour.

She would also spend time with Bob Toski, who she refers to as her "first professional kind of teacher." Bob was at Ocean Reef Club in Key Largo, Florida, and Judy went there for the winter of 1963-1964, mostly playing golf with their guests and working with Toski. Like Mr. Pulver and me, Bob never charged Judy for a lesson.

Judy would eventually meet Walter "Yippy" Rankin. They would marry in 1967 and have a son, Walter Jr., otherwise known as "Tuey," a year later.

That "Best Girl Golfer," in her own words, found "every way to lose." She lost from ahead and she lost from behind until she got her first LPGA win in November 1968, a long, dry spell for someone who was supposed to set the golfing world on fire from the start.

By the time Judy left her playing days behind, she had won 26 times on the LPGA Tour, the last coming in 1981. She was the first player in LPGA history to cross the $100,000 mark in single-season prize money, twice was Player of the Year and three times won the Vare Trophy for the lowest scoring average of the year. She was also a president of the LPGA during her time as a player.

Yippy Rankin.
Photo courtesy of the Solheim Cup

Her barrier-breaking career continues today as she closes in on nearly 40 years in television golf.

Here's our discussion:

DP: Would you say your father was the biggest influence in your young golf life?

JR: Oh, certainly. He started me, and he was a little dogged about it. And I really think a lot it was more what he saw I could do with it (golf).

DP: Mr. Pulver talked about watching you play in the '60s in Florida, mentioning your slight physical stature, the flattest swing he'd ever seen, and a grip that was "simply awful." How did that grip come to be?

JR: My dad and I were at the range about the time I was 7 or 8, and he wanted me to address the ball to look like a man. I have these funky elbows like many women that want to flip up and my dad says "You cannot have the inside of your elbows looking up at the sky. That's how girls play. You need the back of your elbow to look at the target." So the only way I could get my arm to do that was to turn my hand, if that makes sense. Immediately I started hitting the ball considerably farther.

When I was about 14 I went to quite a good teacher in St. Louis, a man named Dave Douglas, and we had decided I would change it (my grip.) He didn't go to moving it a little bit: He went to conventional. I worked and worked for 2½ months or so, trying to do that. I had lost some 25 yards with my seven iron. So he said, "I give." Good for me.

DP: What was your biggest obstacle being a prodigy?

JR: A lot of people don't believe this is true, but I don't think I am inherently competitive. I think if I have to compete I am competitive.

You don't want to convince yourself that they're better than you even though some stand apart. Mickey Wright stood apart. That's not recognizing that they're better than you. That's recognizing that they may be the best.

But I get a kick out of people now that I see that they are so competitive. You know, Brooke Henderson is like this sweetheart of a girl, but she is so competitive.

I think my dad was a Hogan fan, and he wanted me to keep my eyes looking at the ground and concentrate. I think that got me through a lot because I didn't have the most solid nervous system or anything for competing.

DP: Bob Toski. Did you look at him as a mentor and was there something that he consistently reiterated to you?

JR: He didn't try to change my grip. He tried to teach me to play shots with my grip. I think one reason my grip also worked is because I had a good right hand. I'm a proponent of a strong grip today, not what I used to be, but you know Fred Couples has a strong grip, stronger than neutral, but it is not restrictive.

I say beware of teachers who have a theory. Better to just teach some solid stuff. There's somebody who has a quirk, there is that quirk but it's successful and they can repeat it. You know, you don't have to make everybody perfect.

DP: What else about Bob?

JR: I was a really good driver of the golf ball, but Bob tried to make me a good wedge player. I was tolerable. Toski basically taught me a little bit better how to score. We played a course in Biloxi and there was a hole that went that way (left to right) and I just couldn't play that hole. So he got me to where I could hit a little bit of a cut after that.

He also gave me confidence. I was finishing in the top 10 all the time, was a top-10 player, but he said "what we've got to do is figure out how to get you to think you're a winner." It was really hard for me. It was six years before I won.

DP: How did Yippy influence you as a player?

JR: Yippy was very competitive and insisted I be very tough. I believe and I will continue to believe I would not have been successful completely on my own. You might say my father was pushing, and there's a lot of things to say there, but all I know is, even though it was hard, I've ended up in a good place because of him to a great degree.

I'm not sure that I would have achieved without both of them because I'm pretty pliable. I'm a pleaser but I loved finally having Yippy there to argue with. You don't argue with your father. It brought a little something out in me. He got my dander up a lot of times. He didn't know a lot about golf, but he certainly knew everything about competition from a football world and a baseball world. He made me much tougher, no doubt about it. And I think I softened him up a bit.

DP: As a player you broke a lot of barriers and there was a lot of focus on you doing that. What was the hardest part of that time?

JR: It was actually a little easier at that time because Tuey was able to come with us at this point. Yippy was in the insurance business and he could kind of work hard when he was home and then he could come out to meet me. I was really starting to come into my own and figuring out I could win.

I was actually president of the LPGA when I had my two best years. So apparently I was at my best when I was really busy. We were juggling life back home and I was playing pretty good. Here's the other thing: You can't be too self-centered. It is not possible. I think that's sometimes why some of the moms play well on tour; you use your time better and you are not always thinking about yourself.

I probably ran myself into the ground with my back. I had my first incident in 1973. I healed up alright but then I had another pretty bad one in 1975. Once again I healed up, but it was becoming more and more chronic. As the 1970s went on it was apparently taking a bigger toll on me than I thought.

At one time my weight got down to about 103; my good playing weight was about 115. I looked like a skeleton. Yeah, I was clearly playing bad. I was in a bad mood and you know, I'm sure somewhere internally I was considering a nervous breakdown. I truly believe my back had gotten to a point where I couldn't play well again. I had made so many compensations. A few years later, I got the blessings of the job I've had for 35 years.

DP: That brings us to Salem and the 1984 U.S. Women's Open, your first week as a broadcaster. Was there one thing that stood out?

JR: At this point, because of the near nervous breakdown, I could not stand up and talk in front of people. That's a problem. I had what must be close to panic attacks. I just couldn't do it. I always had loved golf on TV, so I went when they asked me, but I didn't know if anything was going to come out (of my mouth).

Fortunately, I knew a number of the people and Rossie (Bob Rosburg) had been my friend. They tell Rossie to take me out there and show me what he does. He took me to three or four different holes, and he said, "I stand here; try to talk so they don't hear you."

The whole thing took about 12 minutes.

He would tell me when I was good or when I was bad and so would Frank Hannigan. I did my first men's U.S. Open in 1985 and this is the great advice they gave me … and they didn't give me too much because I probably would have frozen up. They said we don't want your expertise as a woman. We want your expertise as a golfer.

They (ABC Sports) kind of let me find my way. They humored me and I became a much more confident person. I totally embraced what I was doing. Thanks to ABC Sports for taking a chance on me.

DP: If you had to sum up your broadcast philosophy in one sentence, what would it be?

JR: In the course of a show, try to point out or say something with real meaning or that is impactful a couple times a day. You're not going to do that every time you talk, but it's a couple times a day. You can enlighten somebody or point out something that maybe no one else has noticed. A good broadcast is also coupled with good timing. If you have something really good to say, it is wasted if it is not in the right place in the conversation.

DP: What is the highlight of your broadcasting career or has it even happened yet?

JR: I think it was becoming sort of a fixture at the (British) Open Championship for quite a number of years. It was unbelievable to me where I got to see golf. I was with Tiger (Woods) maybe three or four days when he won at St. Andrews in 2000 and I had a very touching time at St. Andrews with Jack (Nicklaus) in what turned out to be his last round there. It was extraordinary the way people welcomed him. I sometimes slogged around in the worst of the weather, but I brought (Ernie) Els in, I brought (Phil) Mickelson in. Tiger didn't need to be brought in, Dottie, but honestly I can remember some of those shots. I can't remember my own.

You know, it's cool. So I have lived vicariously for a lot of years, through a lot of players, and it's sure been fun.

DP: What is your advice for a woman getting into this crazy television business?

JR: Don't push too hard and you don't have to be like the men you work with; you just have to be capable. I think women are pretty well accepted in almost all corners if they are capable. A man told me a long time ago the only thing wrong with women in the workplace is they keep trying to be like men.

I wanted to write a book so you can use this someday: We were doing the early rounds at Pebble. No, sorry, we were at Torrey Pines. It was the year Tiger won with the broken leg (2008). All of a sudden, I forget where we were on the course, but I look around and realize there are three women out there calling the golf for the No.1, No. 2 and No. 3 players in the world: Woods, Mickelson, and Adam Scott.

I look over and Jane Crafter is calling it for one of the early featured group platforms and Maureen Madill was doing radio. Here we are, three women calling the best players in the world. And I am thinking, oh my gosh, when did this happen? When did it happen that three women are trusted by the public, by the networks, and by these players to call their golf? That should really resonate with you (referring to me). Yeah, you know, when did this happen?

***

Judy Rankin is a pioneer in so many ways, most of which she is too reserved to admit.

She proved you can be a champion on tour while still being a loving mother and wife, a quiet leader on so many levels, and a broadcaster who broke barriers because she was not only capable but kind. Kind to those she worked with and for, but always striving to be better at her trade, openly sharing with those who needed her advice but also clear about what bumps may be in the road. Motherly yet firm.

I had the privilege of twice playing for Judy Rankin on her United States Solheim Cup teams and saw her intense devotion to every player she captained. I've seen her sweat over pairings for those matches while she was, at the same time, making sure her players had clean accommodations and crisply pressed shirts.

She even once told me that I had expended too much energy and I wouldn't be playing an afternoon session in the 1998 Solheim Cup because I needed a nap. She was right — again.

I'm eternally grateful for Judy encouraging me to get into television when I got to that point in my career, much the same as she did — that point where you spend more time rehabbing injuries than improving your game; that point where the game is making life unhappy.

Being beside Judy Rankin in a broadcast booth is a privilege, an opportunity to sponge up her knowledge and experience, just like those years with Mr. Pulver. And I can promise you that in that 2008 U.S. Open, when I picked up the walking coverage of the group of Woods, Mickelson, and Scott as we switched networks, I felt the pressure of following in Judy Rankin's footsteps.

She paved the way for me and so many others, not just in golf, but other sports as well. She did it because she was prepared, capable, and just as she says, "I talk about what I know."

Thank you, Mrs. Rankin.

Looking back on my four years at Furman, I probably studied a little too hard and could have given myself a little more slack in the fun department. Don't get me wrong, I wasn't holed up in some dark corner of the library for my college years. The men's and women's golf teams were a closely knit group and I had plenty of other friends who didn't play sports, many of whom I stay in touch with today. But I operated from a position of fear — afraid my academics weren't going to be enough to keep me in school.

I also had another heavy weight to carry around: I didn't know how to study for anything but an "A." Perfectionism can be such a burden if not managed in a positive way. In fact, the closest I ever came to flunking a course was Introduction to Computer Science. It was one of two pass/fail class options I could select during my four years at Furman and it nearly did me in. I barely skated by.

3-26-84

Dear Mr. Pulver,

I'm sorry it has taken me so long to respond to your letters; school seems to occupy more than enough of my time. My grades are still pretty good. I made a "B," a "B-," and a "B+" during the winter term. I would like to do that well again this term.

My game is starting to come around. I noticed a great deal of improvement at the tournament in Texas two weeks ago and this week I finally cracked the top 10 for the first time. I proved a lot to myself and it feels great to know I can hold my own against the best players in the country. I feel I need to concentrate better and make drastic improvements in my greenside-bunker game, though. The bunkers are really killing me and my confidence in that shot is definately very low. If you have any suggestions - I'd really appreciate it. Other than that, I'm hitting the ball straighter, longer, and better than ever before. The fundamentals you've drilled me on for the past three years have definately been the basis for my steady improvement. I can't thank you enough for that. Having your letters to look back on for reference are an invaluable asset.

Well - schoolwork is calling again so I'll close for now.

I hope things are well with you. Please give my best regards to your family. I'll see you on June 2nd.

Love,
Dottie

P.S. Happy Birthday! ☺

A big change in momentum came for both me and the team at our own invitational, the Lady Paladin, when we won against a strong field and I cracked the top 10 as an individual for the first time in a college event. The Pulver basics were settling in again after the swift kick I gave myself over spring break.

It was not often that Mr. Pulver went into such depth in one letter about a singular part of the physical game, but my whining about bunker play clearly prodded him into making an exception with a lengthy and detailed letter covering every aspect of bunker play and its many variables — from setup to length of shot to different sands.

I was a below-average bunker player (at best) until I had the chance to watch and work with Paul Azinger in 1993. We both represented Head Sportswear at that time, and during a photo shoot at Grand Cypress, we were messing around, hitting bunker shots while the crew set up a new shoot location. Paul was using a 7 iron and getting it closer than I could with my sand wedge.

"Through the years, I have witnessed great sand players, under pressure, look up just before they meet the ball, resulting in a short foozel. So keep your eye on the spot you want to hit, and not the ball." — George Pulver

March 30, 1984

MISS DOTTIE PEPPER
Thurman:

Dottie:

I received your letter and clippings for which I thank you. You
are progressing as fast as you should. In your first year, to get
B's and match shots with the best young women players in our country --
you deserve an accolade.

Now as to bunker shots. I don't think that I was ever a master of the
sand, and during the past four years, I do not recall playing more than
three or fouer bunker shots. However, I shall try to explore some of
the helpful suggestions, that I have gathered along the way.

First sands are all different, when wet or dry, and from experience
and observation you must learn to appraise whaat is before you before
you attempt the shot. Secondly, you must attain superior club head control in entering the sand, that the club head strikes precisely where
your judgement finalized on how little or how much sand should be dis-
turbed. Through the years, I have witness great sand players, under pressure,
look up just before they meet the ball, resulting in a short foozel.
So keep your eye on the spot, you want to hit, and not the ball.

The fundamentals seem to be --and open foot and hip line, that the club
will approach the ball from the outside. In the address the club face
should be aimed at the spot on the green which you feel should be hit, and
not necessarily at the flag. Unlike the big shots, your body should be
open to your flight line, and not parallel to it. About a half swing will
generally suffice, using somewhat early wrist action, but the wrist action
should be firm, and the left hand should guide the swing back and through,
and a firm grip with the left hand may avid one in keeping the blade open
as it enters the sand.

Finally, you must practice this shot a great deal, from different sands,
and distances. Failure to have confidence in recovering from the bunkerside
traps, affects not only the shot getting out, but also the far-away shot into
the green, as no doubt you have observed.

In my view the players who play in the deep South have an advantage. Lots
of uniform sand to practice from. I am less than certain, that the courses
in Saratoga, have uniform and well prepared traps. The sand at McGregor
is very fine, and packs fom a rain or sprinkler in operation. Perhaps they
have hauled-in more uniform sand since I left.

My family is well thank you, but widely dispersed. I just talked with Jean
in Atlanta, and George in Catskill, and all seems well. Madelyn has been
in Hawaii, for two weeks on business, but I understand she is flyinging back
to California today.

George

P. S. Anytime you observe a really fine trap artist at work, try to sneak
some of her magic, from her methods. In the long run you will have to learn
the best method for you. HOW IS YOUR LEFT WRIST?

It wasn't until then that I fully grasped, fully felt what Mr. Pulver wrote about keeping the blade open as it enters the sand. Paul talked about having your left hand's "knuckles up," not letting the club release. It only took me nine years; quick learner, I am!

Mr. Pulver was a believer in observing the best players' techniques — watch "the best do what they do best" — and I have followed suit. As an announcer, one of my favorite things is to watch players warm up on the practice area, hit bunker shots, and putt — not to interrupt with conversation or take them out of their routines but hear the sounds, watch the body language, see trends in good shot shapes and misses.

I was fortunate to be able to pick Zinger's brain on bunker play, but I also learned an enormous amount watching Joanne Carner and Jeff Sluman hit bunker shots. Part setup, part technique, part artistry, all resulted in the wonderful "thump" when they struck shot after shot from every bunker lie imaginable.

Our Furman team went into the NCAA Championship at the Innisbrook resort in Florida on a roll, and I had also continued to play better with the back-to-basics philosophy, winning individually in a playoff at Duke, followed by another top 10 in the lead-up to the National Championship. We would ultimately finish third behind the powerhouse programs of Miami and Arizona State. It was another "Little Engine That Could" story for a school whose enrollment was less than 3,000 students.

Mr. Pulver always said you would learn a lot about yourself and how you handle pressure by continually putting yourself in those situations; learn how your head reacts, he said, and how your body reacts. Well, I learned a lot that week, because I was in the hunt for the individual title from Day 1, hanging tough until the last hole, where it looked like I needed to hole out for eagle to tie. I fired it right at the flag and then four-putted from 15 feet above the hole to finish T-5. I spent part of every pre-round warmup sick with nerves in the bathroom and closed it out with four putts at the last. Clearly, I was not ready yet. His "take things slow and check every box along the way" philosophy was right yet again.

I didn't achieve my super-long-shot goal of making the Curtis Cup team, but there were many positives to take from the first year of college. It was now time to focus on finally leaving junior golf with another win while also trying to qualify for the Women's Open.

When I returned home and to the lesson tee with Mr. Pulver, I had one of those sessions where his follow-up letter just didn't resonate with me. We didn't have many but this was one of those rare disconnects. He reiterated how the right knee must drive to the target. But for me, thinking with my left side always seemed to connect better. Others would say they learn best with a right-side feel or picture in their brain.

Regardless, I find it amusing that he would say toward the end of his letter that he had used too many words and to "just keep doing what you are doing."

"Legs seem to start the downswing, hips follow, and finally the large shoulder muscles unwind late." — George Pulver

June 6, 1984

DOTTIE:

GJP

First let me say it was nice to work with you again, and must exclaim, you
are hitting the ball magnificently, and you look very well. College and Golf
seems to agree with you.

Lets go directly to your golf --

These things you well know -- "The most important move in starting back is
to come back low and sloly, about straight back, but not outside unless you
want to fade the ball. Should one start back too fast, the best hand and arm,
goes to work too   early, and the club is lifted, and the turn is semi-lost,
because the large pivoting muscles do not have a chane to get the club back
into the plane of your swing, which must be determine by your height, and the
distance you stand from the ball.

The most important thing in starting down is to drive the right knee toward your
target, so that you weight moves first. This does two thing which I am sure
you are aware of, it get you down on and inside arc, and even more importantly,
delays the release of your hand and wrist action, that the club will have tremendous acceleration meeting the ball. I have found that many pupils when starting
down, do not respond too well with moving the left leg first. Others get the
proper down swing by starting the hips toward the target. After much thought,
I am still convinced there is a push-off with the right leg which gets the
mechanism working. Legs seem to start the downswing, hips follow, and finally
the large shoulders muscles unwind late. But don't get too mental about it.
Just find a way in which your shoulders unwind late, and your hand action comes
from the inside, with a last minute release.

Already, too many damn words. Just keep doing what you are doing. For the life
of me I failed to come up with any specifics. After watching you hit out of that
mud, I feel that your mention of hitting now and then to the right, or high and
loss of distance to be caused by the sudden too early use of your shoulders and
hands starting down. In other words your push off lookswell, but it is sort of
feeble
Your schedule is intelligent.

Good luck, and anytime you may want what limited help I may be able to give
call on me. The trouble lies in the fact that a golfer cannot see himself,
and must go by feel. He or she is often wrong.

Please say hello tour father and Mother,

The best player-teacher combinations seem to have their own language. How the teacher relays information through the words and techniques is a big deal, and what works for one most certainly will not work for all. What is important, though, is to find that personal code, that language and action that gets the best out of each other. Mr. Pulver gave me the permission to find out what worked best for me and, in fact, insisted on it.

While the right knee driving to the target may not have worked for me toward the beginning of the letter, what did hit home and become a checkpoint through my entire career was his comment about a "feeble" push off. Whenever my lower body got lazy, I was in trouble. These were more seeds sown for long-term growth, self-reliance, and understanding of my swing.

Before the summer golf schedule kicked into overdrive, I was asked by Ralph Montoya, easily one of the most charismatic and best-playing professionals in our area, to help him give a junior clinic at his club in the southern portion of our PGA Section. We ended around noon, and with the U.S. Open being held at Winged Foot, just over an hour from Ralph's club, he put his PGA member's badge in my hand with the orders to take advantage of being in the vicinity. He said to park as close as that badge would get me and watch the players on the range on this last day of practice before the championship began. Ralph knew my golfing idol was Seve Ballestros and maybe, if I got really lucky, I could watch him practice.

Seve Ballestros. Photo courtesy of Frank Christian/PGA of America, 1989

So, off Mom and I went, going south to Winged Foot instead of north toward home. That magical badge got us a parking spot right beside the driving range. And who was the first player I saw? Seve! I spent 30 minutes watching every swing he made, mesmerized, even though he was hitting balls right next to then current Masters champion Ben Crenshaw. Seve was my guy, the only player to have his picture on my cork board at home. Flamboyant, handsome, dashing, and bit of a rebel, he was it for me. Unfortunately, a wicked thunderstorm cut short my time watching him practice. But in a mere 30 minutes, I was inspired for the entire summer and, frankly, for my entire career.

I was inspired by Seve the same way I knew Mr. Pulver was inspired by players he had watched, from Ray to Vardon, Collett to Rankin, Sarazen to Jones, Nicklaus to Trevino and beyond. I got the lesson, big time.

Leaving junior golf with a convincing win at the AJGA event at Stratton and then qualifying for the U.S. Women's Open two days later set the tone for a summer that would change my playing opportunities for the rest of my time as an amateur.

In another letter to Lou Torre of the *Gazette,* Mr. Pulver paid me an enormous compliment, one that stuck with me as much as many of the swing thoughts he passed along: "… she did not shrink from sweat and toil."

June 29, 1984

Lou Torre,
Schenectady Gazette.
Schenectady. N. Y.

Dear Lou:

Hello and I trust everything goes well with you.
I did indeed appreciate your recent column onDottie Pepper.

My help to Dottie has been small. She deserves all the credit
for her advancement. In my humble opinion she has the most
glorious swing, man or women, that I have seen in our area in
sixty years. However, a champion must have more and she has--
a great heart, the supreme dedication to advance her golf. and
she does not shrink from sweat and toil.

Lou, you too are a champion. A master golf scribe, who after
twenty-five years, continue to hold and enthrall Golfers with
your column.

Lou, please no reply.

George J. Pulver,

P. S. Copy to Dottie:

Over the next couple of weeks, we would sweat and toil in preparation for that trip to the Women's Open, not just physically and psychologically but Mr. Pulver would also teach me the nuances of Donald Ross' architectural style at Salem and, after that, also made sure I grasped the magnitude of the history made there when Babe Zaharias won the 1952 U.S. Women's Open by 12 shots, just 18 months after undergoing cancer surgery. Mr. Pulver wanted me to be prepared for the course but also to be inspired by its history. It was thorough and complete preparation.

By the time I got to Salem, the only big surprise was my 7:09 a.m. tee time Thursday. I'd played plenty of early golf but never that early in a tournament round. Mr. Pulver had prepared me for the long rough and greens that would likely be rock-hard by the weekend, the need to be creative with my short game, to look at the best players in an effort to learn but not to be overly awed, to dig deeper than I ever had before. By that Sunday night, I was low amateur in the U.S. Women's Open, tying for 22nd overall, which gave me access to tournaments I had only read about or watched on television. And it got my foot in the door for the 1986 Curtis Cup. I remember calling Mr. Pulver before leaving Peabody to share the great news. He, for the first time, was essentially speechless.

That low amateur honor and tournament access also came with more anxiety for my parents as it qualified me for the U.S. Women's Amateur in Seattle, most definitely not a drive trip. To this day I still don't know where the money for that airplane ticket and week in Seattle came from, although I have a strong suspicion that my grandparents paid for it.

Dottie is congratulated for being the low amateur in the 1984 U.S. Women's Open. Photo courtesy U.S. Golf Association.

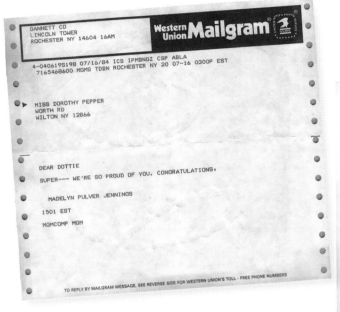

A congratulatory Mailgram to Dottie from Madelyn, George Pulver's daughter.

WOMEN'S AMATEUR CHAMPIONSHIP

OF THE

UNITED STATES GOLF ASSOCIATION

PLAYERS' DINNER

SATURDAY, AUGUST 11, 1984

BROADMOOR GOLF CLUB

SEATTLE, WASHINGTON

RECEPTION 6:15 P.M.   DINNER 7:00 P.M.

NOT TRANSFERABLE

Player should present this to Registration Committee at Club where Championship is held.

PLAYER'S CERTIFICATE
84th United States Women's Amateur Championship
Conducted by the United States Golf Association

This is to certify that . . Dottie Pepper . . . .

player's name

is eligible to compete for the Championship, having qualified at . fully exempt . . . .

name of qualifying section

Certified by official in charge of Sectional Qualifying Rounds:

Signed . . . .

Address . . . . Telephone . . . .

City . . . .

State . . . . Zip code . . . .

 Important notice on other side

Dottie's certificate for the U.S. Women's Amateur Championship at Broadmoor Golf Club.

Dottie, center, with her sister Jackie at left and cousin Alicia after the Gazette Women's Amateur championship.

August 1, 1984

MISS DOTTIE PEPPER,
Box, 196,
Worth Road,
Gansevoort, N. Y. 12831

DOTTIE:

In winning at Rexford -- You were just magnificient. No one but a student of golf can ever know the inward agony, that you endured.

Of all the great players that I have seen in my lifetime, few had flawless swings, but they all had the matchless desire to Win. A champion has this something else.

I enclose an article which ponders the undieing goal, that leaders in all fields possess. You shall often win, and frequently lose. So What! Its manner in which your search for excellence, remains to the very end.

Before you go West, I would like to see you briefly at the range, at your convenience.

P. S.   Say hello to your father and Mother.

I'd defend the Gazette title by birdieing the final hole, prompting this letter of August 1st with an accompanying article highlighting the qualities of exceptional leaders, emphasizing the way they search for excellence.

The Tour

tues '84

THE UNDRIVEN

In the case of some players,
the fire doesn't burn quite as hot

"Dottie please do not return"

by MIKE BRYAN

Standing on the 14th tee during that incredible final round of the British Open at Turnberry in 1977, Jack Nicklaus and Tom Watson exchanged glances.

"This is what it's all about, Jack, isn't it?" Watson asked.

"It sure is" was the reply.

The highest stakes, fierce competition, mental pressure unknown to most of us, the culminating challenge of years of work and dedication —what it must be all about for a professional golfer, right?

Wrong. Some pro golfers don't like the heady but thin air at the top of Mt. Everest, or the struggle to get there. They aren't interested in being the next Nicklaus or Watson. Or they're not good enough and know it.

They are the undriven—and they're not ashamed of it.

Johnny Miller, one of the most successful undrivens, says, "I don't want to be a big, important person with all those demands on my time. There are only a few of the truly insatiable —Nicklaus, Watson, Palmer, Player. Ninety per cent of us may *say* how much we want it, but deep down . . ."

Pro golfers aren't that much different from the rest of us. They may seek inspiration from all the books and cassette tapes on motivation they want, but if the drive is not in their hearts, it doesn't matter what's in their heads. Talk comes cheap. The real commodity is expensive.

Undriven Gary McCord argues that rationalization is necessary for all but the greatest players. A defense against losing, he believes, is vital because "the Tour is not a winning

atmosphere. There is so much losing out here. We all get beaten week after week. We all have to learn to live with defeat."

Although Nicklaus has lost many more times than he has won, it's doubtful that he has ever learned to "live with defeat." The driven live with winning; losing for them is an aberration that won't last.

Living with winning did not prove so vital for Bill Rogers. In 1981, the skinny Texan won seven times around the world, including the British Open and the World Series. He sped all over the place that fall and winter, cashing in. In 1982, he burned out and has won once since that great year.

"I didn't want to pay the price," Rogers conceded later. The drive just is not there. He doesn't apologize, and sees nothing wrong with "cruising along, winning occasionally."

A key point: The money in and around golf is so good today that quick success engenders quick riches. Miller was fixed for life after a few great years, a Sears clothing endorsement and other windfalls that resulted. Bobby Clampett made a bundle after his 1982 campaign, which included a victory, a tie for third in the U.S. Open and the much-publicized disaster at the British Open, which he led by five shots after two rounds.

It's harder to be driven with money in the bank. Dave Marr: "With quite a few of the pros, it seems they want to be just moneymakers."

At the very least, the money separates the truly driven from the merely ambitious.

So does talent. Gary Koch realizes that, at this stage of his career (eight years on Tour), he is not "the next Nicklaus." No use kidding himself. "I'm a driven kind of person, but I'm realistic. The next Nicklaus has to be winning majors by the time he's 25 or 26. I'm older than that and I haven't won a major yet. That level of greatness doesn't fit my self-image."

Koch, one of the more thoughtful and articulate pros, endured a five-year victory drought between 1978 and last year, when he captured Doral. This year, he's added two more titles, San Diego and Bay Hill.

While being the greatest player in the game is not part of Koch's self-image, neither is being a non-winner. "For those bad years, I was out of my 'comfort zone,' on the lower end. I expected to be better than I was," Koch says.

Likewise Jack Renner, who had good campaigns in 1982 and '83 but considered them "disappointing." He admits, "I hadn't been going out of my way to dedicate myself." Renner is an interesting case of a player driven to win golf tournaments and prove his talent but basically uninterested in the power and glory that go along with it.

Peter Oosterhuis says of Renner: "He might win $500,000 and still not be a superstar because he might not allow it. It's against his nature."

Koch and Renner are driven to be as good as they think they can be —but not better. The danger of this pragmatic approach, Koch acknowledges, is that while avoiding unattainably high goals, the golfer may sell

continued

Illustration by Chris Notarile

A one-on-one session with Mr. Pulver

These four snapshots were, to the best of my recollection, taken in late summer 1984 by Madelyn at Duffer's Den, just prior to my return to Furman. We were trying to sort out the best makeup of my bag before returning to school.

As he offered in his June 6 letter to me that year, "… anytime you may want what limited help I may be able to give, call on me." This was a perfect example of that help.

Most of our lessons were late morning or early afternoon as Mr. Pulver loved keeping his hand in the agronomy at Brookhaven earlier in the day. Most lessons lasted a bit over an hour, but we never had a fixed end-time. We worked until he felt we had made the necessary progress. He was not one to lean heavily on drills in the full swing but on hitting different shots to varied targets.

Our sessions could be best described as focused and detailed while still very personal. I would often talk about situations that had popped up in tournament rounds, ask about how to play certain shots, share my goals, and, of course, the frustrations I had as well. I cannot recall him ever being frustrated with me, although sometimes he was frustrated by trying to find the right words to get through my thick head.

It was always purposeful time spent and, without fail, ended on an encouraging, positive note, often with another lesson scheduled.

He wasn't there to kill time. Because of his example, neither was I.

Well-rounded preparation, not just golf preparation, was of great importance to Mr. Pulver, something I believe is all too often lost in today's ultra-competitive and lucrative world of youth sports. Give me the kid who has balance on and away from the field 10 out of 10 times over those early specializers who so often burn out too soon.

The trip to Seattle started out with a comfortable enough walk through stroke play qualifying with a tie for 6th place and a high seed in match play, but I was beaten in the first round by North Carolina State's Leslie Brown. This loss further cemented my dislike of match play because even with Leslie's bomb for birdie and the win on the 18th hole, I had beaten her in total strokes for the day. It was not until Joanne Carner's simple advice for a successful match play mentality ("Just go win the first hole") was delivered 10 years later that I really embraced and loved match play.

Mr. Pulver offered his condolences about the loss … but only briefly.

August 17, 1984

MISS DOTTIE PEPPER
Box 196, Worth Road,
Gansevoort N. Y. 12831

Dottie:

I am indeed sorry, that you did not win, but all competitors must learn to lose as well as win.

Temporary you have been turned back -- put out on the Eighteenth by an heroic putt. Pause for a moment, and reflect the innumeral instances, you too have snatched victory on the final holes. I have learned the inscrutable power which so often controls our destonies, evenly allots his favors in the long run. Be patient!

Welcome home. When you feel like resuming your golf call me. I would like to see your beautiful swing again.

Finally, no brooding! Continue your plans with undiminished determination. I predict many successes lie before you.

George,

P. S. Say hello to your Father and Mother.

October 4 1984

Miss Dottie Pepper
Furman University,
P. O. Box 27934
Greenville S. C.   29613

Dottie:

This date under another cover, I am sending you a book, which you
may enjoy. As the days and months drone on, please charge my silence,
to a sore foot, and the apathy that comes with the years.

This book, "Thirty years of Golf" by Sarazen. I am persuaded that a golfer
of your skill, can gain an immense good from time to time picking it up.

First, Herbert Warren Wind co-author, pens his golf tales in poetry of
words, much the same as Grantland Rice did to his football greats.
Secondly, by his own incisive words, Sarazen uncovers the mental drive
which separates a champion from the runner-up.

Too many books on golf touch only upon the mechanics. I feel, as soon
as one roughly gets his swing, more than 60% of his or her success, de-
pends on the mental attitudes.

When you return next summer, be good enough to return the Sarazen book.

Hang-in-there!

George

P. S. Your sweater gift is a beauty. My son took one look at it, and
remarked "Come March, it shall go with me to Vail for Spring skiing.
By the way, Bert Edwards, is certainly one of your staunchest admiriers.
in our area. When he comes across scraps of information on you, I learn
of them. That "Golf World" which I recently mailed you, came from Bert.

As summer moved on and I returned to school at Furman, I noticed my mentor beginning to fail a bit, and his feet and hands beginning to bother him. By the spring, I would have to tell him where shots went on the range because his eyesight became a challenge. Even so, I still couldn't slip a marginal shot past him. His hearing was always perfect. He didn't need to see where the practice balls went, he could hear where they went.

The book he referenced was a suggested second reading of Gene Sarazen's *Thirty Years of Championship Golf*. The book does spend time, as I knew from the first time around, on fundamentals and mechanics but it also digs deeper into the mental strength of great champions. He must have felt I needed an extra helping of those reminders, and I re-read the book through that filter. It certainly sunk in because I won the following week in Memphis and finished second in Destin shortly thereafter. This book was also among those given to me by the Pulver family after his passing. Such a gift.

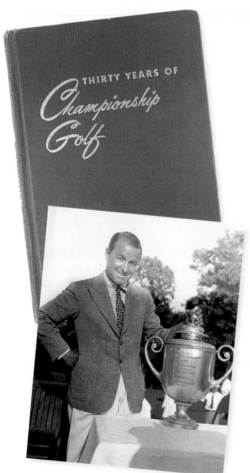

At age 86, Mr. Pulver was beginning to slow physically but his mind and attention to the details of top performance were not. It was almost as if he had a running checklist of things he felt I needed to be aware of, or in this case, maybe he was in his back shed on a mid-October day fiddling with grips and felt he needed to make me more aware of their importance.

After receiving this letter, I remember ordering new grips and two-way grip tape as well as lighter fluid and a super-sharp knife. From then through college, I changed my own grips. I often changed them in my dorm room on campus, which was not exactly to the delight of my roommate, Elizabeth Belcher, but she was patient and understanding beyond belief.

The club he refers to in this letter is a 3 wood he made for me before I left for school in September. It was a PowerBilt Citation head he had in his workshop, fit with a stronger Dynamic Gold B shaft. It was sort of a stopgap as I continued to gain strength and needed to upgrade equipment.

Gene Sarazen with the Wanamaker Trophy at the 1933 PGA Championship. George Pulver, Sr., also qualified for the championship.

Saturday, October 13, 1984

Dottie:

I was happy to get your letter, but please undersand, I know the
pressures you are under. Three of my children all graduated from
good unniversities, and they had only the normal amount of brains,
and they scrambled.

I am delighted to learn that your electives were well chosen. In this
life you may find the need of being not only a fine golfer, but a thinking one as well.

The girls from those Southern Colleges, are tough to follow, but hang in
there. They are the pick of the land in golf, many have been playing since
almost infancy, strong muscles, are only those which have been tested.

From the press, and otherwise, I keep appraised of your efforts, and I
know of none, who have gone so far, in her field.

I have never spoken to you of new grips, but I know most of the tour
players, regrip almost every year, at least, the clubs that you use
so often. There are two thing about grips. They help one retain control of the clubs, but even more importantly, with time they wear, and
become microscopically thinner, and a different feel results.

One day, as you become stronger, you may have to move up to a stronger
shaft, but don't hasten it. The men's R shafts are lighter, and have more
feel, and the first place you will find benefit from using a strong shaft,
is in a club like a #3 wood, because of the turf resistance. When the time
comes for a stronger shaft, be aware that you shall probably not hit the
ball any farther, but more often straighter. I think that #3 wood, to be
an excellent club, for one of your skill, and hand strength.

I am doing fine thank you, just doddering more. Indian summer is upon us,
and its a pleasant respit, before the storms.

George J.

Pass along a word of chear to your father and mother. Be advised that
you have a lot of admirers here in Saratoga, and you deserve them.

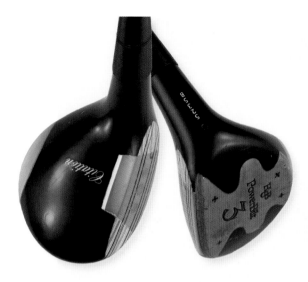

That 3 wood is still in my office today.

Mr. Pulver's final letter of the year centered on a January 1984 Golf Digest article about Jack Nicklaus and the keys to his swing, one that had evolved throughout his career but stayed true to its basics. Mr. Pulver was a fan of Nicklaus, not only because of how his length and strength transformed the game at that time but perhaps even more so because of his mental strength.

Two words jump off the page: "personally perfect." He truly believed there is no best swing for all, and I agree wholeheartedly. Mr. Pulver forbid me from reading the instruction articles in the golf publications, not wanting my brain to be over cluttered with mechanics. But at the same time, through his endless curiosity about the game, he exposed me to many thoughts and golf swings. I was so fortunate that he didn't have a cookie-cutter teaching philosophy, a one-dimensional look at the golf swing, or a rigid definition of a champion.

With today's technology it would be so easy to lay digital imaging over a player and say, "OK, this is how you must swing the club" when in fact the best teachers are pushing the envelope of "personally perfect," using the technology to help their students be their best in their most natural and repeatable way. Players like Dustin Johnson, Bryson DeChambeau, Jim Furyk, and Matthew Wolff, teachers like the Harmon brothers, Boyd Summerhays, Chris Como, George Gankas — they've all found their own "personally perfect" way to swing and teach. Mr. Pulver would have loved that.

I chuckle when I read the foreshadowing in this final letter of the year where Mr. Pulver talked about Nicklaus' determination still being undiminished, having won just twice on the PGA Tour since winning two major championships in 1980. He had a hunch that Nicklaus and what he termed his "hypnotic concentration" weren't done just yet. Sure enough, Mr. Pulver was right about that, too. Jack, with son Jackie on the bag, would in 16 months turn back the clock, winning the Masters for a sixth time, at age 46.

Mr. Pulver was also beginning to subtly tell me that I needed to be stronger in finding my own way because his health was becoming a bigger issue. It had been a year that would open many competitive opportunities in the future, a year that affirmed so much of what we had worked on. His advice from the start had been to keep things simple, to play as much locally and regionally with other bits of competition sprinkled in as it came. It all stacked up better than I could have imagined, and I couldn't wait to get at it in the new year ahead.

December 10, 1984

DOTTIE:

Hello and how are you?

This letter is prompted by an article by Nichlaus, in the January edition of "Golf Digest" which no doubt you have seen. I don't think that you could improve the swing that you were using, because the swing that you were using was so personally perfect. In my view, your philosophy, your composure, your desire to excell -- these are the factors that can lead you upwards.

About three years ago, Nichlaus for the first time stried to overhaul his swing. He began to realize that to keep up with the improving young golfers, he had to flatten his swing, and come more from in-to-out to retain his power. Then too, his vision was failing, and he now is helped by the young eyes of his son, his caddie.

The first time I saw Nichlaus play, was out at Cornell, during the Intercollegiat His power was awesome, his desire to win, unequaled, and his concentration hypnotic.

Nichlaus's determination to excel remains undiminished. His desire to win, still a burning flame. Certainly, he will have to give up his throne, to the young, but he shall never accept it, until forced to.

No big changes but keep tyying to improve what you have. There is no best swing for all. Go with what you have, and which comes natural for you. Your swing and courses change with the years, as well as your physiology, so some evolving must take place.

Sincerely,

Roger Maltbie, Dottie Pepper and Brandie Burton at the 1994 Solheim Cup.
Photo courtesy of LPGA archives.

"I'm eternally grateful for Judy encouraging me to get into television when I got to that point in my career, much the same as she did — that point where you spend more time rehabbing injuries than improving your game; that point where the game is making life unhappy." – Dottie Pepper

Dottie, Sandra Haynie, Yippy and Judy Rankin.
Photo courtesy of J.C. Penney LPGA Skins Game.

TOURNAMENT RECORD

1984 - (Age 18-19)

- T-4 Betsy Rawls Invitational, Great Hills C.C.

- T-9 Lady Paladin Invitational, Furman University Golf Course

- Winner, Duke Spring Invitational, Duke University Golf Course

- 6th place, Fall Creek Falls Invitational, Memphis State University, Fall Creek Falls Golf Course

- T-5 NCAA Women's Championship, Innisbrook Resort Island Course

- Winner, AJGA Northern Junior, Stratton Mountain Golf Course

- Lost in second round, Women's Western G.A. Championship, New Haven C.C.

- T-22 U.S. Women's Open, Salem C.C. (low amateur)

- Winner, Gazette Women's Amateur Championship, Edison Club

- T-6 stroke play qualifying, lost in first round of match play U.S. Women's Amateur Championship, Broadmoor Golf Course

- Winner, Memphis Women's Intercollegiate, Stonebridge C.C.

- AJGA Second Team Junior All-American

Chapter 6

While 1984 had been a banner year in so many ways, there was a late-season challenge: a severe left ankle injury during a racquetball game, complicated by the onset of synovitis in the joint capsule. It was a swollen, painful mess; air cast, crutches, all of it. I went at everything to the max, so why not play racquetball that way and approach rehab in the same manner?

It would be nearly two months before I was back to 100 percent, but Mr. Pulver used that down time to explain the differences in my new clubs and the materials used in them, further building my equipment knowledge, and to focus on my short game. Use a challenge to better yourself; be ready to go full tilt when your body allows.

The gem in this letter is in one line buried near the end: "Do not play all of your short shots with a wedge." There is no substitute for creativity in the game, and it's so important to learn how to play every shot with every club. I inwardly cheer when I see players today grab for clubs other than their wedges, putting the ball on the ground quicker, and getting the ball to react like a putt on the green. Certainly, a particular wedge might be your favorite in the bag, but a complete player can play the shots with any club.

The 9 iron was my favorite for the simple short shots, but learning how to control the flight and reaction of the ball by position in the stance and manipulating the club face or even changing your grip, is artistry — reliable artistry and repetition that does not break down in the heat of battle. That artistry can turn a sand wedge into a 6 iron and vice versa. Mr. Pulver believed that made a complete player — a completely prepared player.

In mid-January Mr. Pulver was hospitalized for a couple of weeks. I don't recall the diagnosis but it was very difficult for him. He liked to be active, fiddling in his shed, staying up on the latest in the game and the news around town.

Dottie in 1985 at the Gail Sykes Best Ball Championship, Ballston Spa C.C. She won the tournament in a playoff. Photo courtesy of the Gazette.

NEW YEARS DAY, 1985

DEAR DOTTIE:

It was nice to see you prior to NEW YEARS. I trust that you
and your family arrived to School all safely. After you left with
your new shining clubs I felt I should address myself more completely to your questions. First, I hasten to say, I am no expert
ongraphyte heads. I have however,fooled aroundgraphyte shafts for
about ten years.

At this point of time, I urge you to to keep an open opinion, in
this matter, until by trial and error you have become more convinced.
A graphyte inserted into a wood head, produces a club nearly the same
SWT., but less dead weight. Therefore less dead weight, less energy
would be required to obtain the same speed. Some mass is lost.

On the other hand, when steel is inserted into graphyte,more weight
may be needed to bring up the club head mass. Alarger head is therefore
being used, to capture additional mass, and weight added to the inside perimeter of head to the same end, and balance. Over the years,
I have found, time is neededm when new materials come into use.

And finally in the end, select the set that you feel most comfortable
and confident in using. And trust your own judgement. Your natural style,
and it is a good one, is virtually set. Change reluctantly, but only after
much pondering.

Sincerely,

P. S. Try the new clubs three or four weeks then please write me. You
will have to get use to the larger head of the Driver. You may find the
need to address the smaller #4 Wood, slightly heelward. With use, the SWT
of that Driver may need to lose a point or two. Yousr ankle may force you
to cut down slightly in your practice. Get after your short shots, and putting.
Don't play all of your short shots with a wedge. THE SET OF IRONS SHOULD
CAUSE YOU LITTLE CONCERN.

Being hospitalized during the darkest days of winter was extraordinarily tough. His kids as well as my parents visited, but it was my job to increase my correspondence, keeping his focus moving forward.

There was plenty to write about with equipment choices, updates on classes, weather challenges, winter collegiate rankings, and tournaments on the schedule — all things he loved hearing about and being able to offer his knowledge and opinions. There was also the happy news of an unanticipated trip home to accept an award, the Empire State Plaza Collegiate Athlete of the Year, in mid-February. It was perfect timing to be able to be with him after his release from the hospital and before our spring schedule would begin at Furman.

So, I sent along two letters, both aimed at lifting his spirits.

Furman University
GREENVILLE, SOUTH CAROLINA

January 17, 1985

Dear Mr. Pulver—

Hi!! I heard about your trip to the hospital yesterday and I can only hope it will a short and successful stay -- I know how much you like anything to do with doctors and hospitals! Knowing you you'll be out of there and back to normal as soon as you can. I hope you're feeling better by the time you get this letter.

It was very nice to get your letter last week. My ankle is getting better and my golf is pretty good, too. Two days ago I got new irons from Titleist. They're even better than the Yamaha's I showed you when I was home over Christmas. They came with 3 wedges: a 49° pitching wedge, a 54° pitching wedge and a 59° sand wedge. I'm not sure which pitching wedge to use -- do you have any suggestions? I will probably keep using my own sand wedge that you filed for me right before I came to school in September. It's a Titleist anyway and I've had really good results with it all year.

School is going pretty well -- lots of work and too few hours in a day, but I suppose everyone feels like that once in a while. I'm taking Financial Accounting, Principles of Coaching and a Philosophical Bases class that is an indepth study of careers in Physical Education. I have a big paper due in that class on the 30th.

I'm doing it on the role of law in physical education. So far, its very interesting. Next week I have to set up my classes for the spring term, but I don't know what I'm going to take yet.

So, how is the weather up there? Mom has told me it has been rather cold. It's been cold here, too. Last night we got some ice and snow, but it will be gone by dinner-time. Most of the schools around here are closed today, but not good ol' Furman. I was definitely hoping school would be closed today.

The national rankings came out for collegiate golf two days ago. I'm ranked fourth in the nation individually and the team is ranked fourteenth. I was pleased with my individual ranking, but not the team ranking. We'll have to improve on that in order to go to the NCAA Championship in Cape Cod at the end of May. Some more good news: I was picked as the Empire State Plaza Collegiate Athlete of the Year (the same award I got as a high school athlete.) The dinner is Feb 12 at the Best Western in Albany and the selection committee is flying me home for it on the 11th. I'm real excited about it. There should be a press release in the papers soon. I'll be home until the 13th so you can definitely expect to see me!

Well— I have to go to class and put this in the mail so I guess I'd better sign off for now. I'll write again tomorrow or Saturday. Hang in there & get better real soon. (Don't give those nurses and doctors a hard time either! ☺)

I'll see you on Feb. 12th.

All my love,
Dottie

1-20-85

Dear Mr. Puner,

Hi!!! I've got a few spare minutes before I have to leave for church so I thought I'd use the time to check in to see how you are doing. I hope you're feeling better – you certainly have been on my mind alot!

Everything here is going pretty well. I've gotten alot of school work done in the past 3 days and feel much better about that. By tonight I will be through with the research for my paper that's due on the 30th. It's really going to be a good one!

At noon today the men's and women's golf team are getting together for a brunch. It should be a lot of fun. After that I'll have to go straight to the library so I can watch the Super Bowl and the Phoenix Open on TV later today. I'm hoping Calvin Peete can make a come-back after losing his big lead yesterday.

Well– it's about time I got going. I'll write more when I get back.

Bye!

JIM DAVIS

GARFIELD Characters: ©1978 United Feature Sy

11:30 PM

I talked to mom about two hours ago and she had some good news for me – she said you're doing alot better and are getting anxious to get back home again. That's great! Keep it up!

I got alot of my work done today – spent 3½ hours in the library working on my paper and worked on my accounting until about 10 minutes ago when I decided to quit.

We're suffering through a major cold snap down here. It's 3 degrees outside right now. Tomorrow's high is expected to be 20° and Tuesday doesn't look much better. No golf for a few days! It looks like Florida is even getting hit with the cold weather. Both the men's and women's golf coaches here are at the PGA Golf Show in Orlando this weekend. They'll be be back Tuesday.

Well– I'm getting real tired so I think I'm going to get to bed. Keep up the great progress –

I'll be thinking about you! See you in 3 weeks.

Love, always,
Dottie

It was beginning about this time that I'd noticed changes in his typing and the way he communicated on paper — signs that he was facing new challenges. There were many good days but more that were a struggle. Eight weeks of lousy health, short daylight hours, and medicine he didn't really like made for some really trying times. Writing, as he says, "has become a chore for me, so please overlook my scrambles." The writing may have been a chore, but he was still on point about the importance of good alignment and being committed to a consistent shot shape.

Jan. 24, 1985

Dear Dottie:

I enjoyed your letter of the 18th. If I appear to respond with lethargy,
please charge it to my health for the past eight weeks. The pills etc.,
which they hand me , is trying to say the least. I shall try to improve.

Allignment sometimes comes slowly, Generally speaking the foot line and
the foot line in a full shot is generally parallel. to the target line
in the address or about parallel. Yet a great player such as Snead
used a slightly closed stance with the full shots. Wonderful Nachslaus
stoods slightly open when he went for power, because of his Upright Swing.
Time will tell your one way or the other, but stay very close to square.
Except for specil shots, a slight fade, a small draw,or nearly straight
could be used.   Follow your confidence in this matter.

On your full swings, stay very close to square, to start with, and be
led by confidence in deciding the best way for you to attack a ball.

As you no doubt observe, writing has become a chore for me, so please overlook
my scrambles.

                    Sincerely,

                    George J. Pulver.

P.S. A word of cheer to your Father & Mother

GEORGE J. PULVER
136 EAST AVENUE
SARATOGA SPRINGS, NEW YORK 12866

February 5, 1985

Dear Dottie:

I was delighted to get your letter of Jan. 23rd.

Writing a short note has never been a chore but recently
I have not felt up to it. I offer this excuse in defense
of my silence to to your cheerful letters and kind notes.

I am taken over with the feeling that most difficult year in
college to be the Second year. So hang in there to the very
end, as you have been forced to do in your golf matches.

Now to Golf -- Spring Bermuda greens are terrible tough,
but you say always to the right. Frozen Bermuda cannot be ~~the trouble~~
the trouble.

You may be changing the tension of your grip during the stroke.
Tightening the grip just at impact is a No, No.

Putting to the right is generally caused by a slightly closed
stance, or taking the club too much inside going back, or even
bad alignment, top-of blade too open at the address. In putting
to the left, the cause may be picking up he head, as the putter
goes back.

Watch the grip of your left hand, that the knuckles face the target in the address, and not the earth.

A slightly diferent Putter may help mentally.

Try different grips and search for one, that get the ball where
you want it. Generally the foot line should go straight at the
hole. However, a slight turn of the hips, either to the left
or right works for some.

I suggest that you putt again and again from about three feet
from the hole, then move back to four feet. Watch for a pattern
of where the ball ends, on the right or left side of the hole.

I hope to see you as the house for a few minutes as you pass
by. I am sorry that I shall not be able to attend your party
but promise me that you shall face your honors with your head
carried high, and with the knowledge you got where you are with
anguish, sweat and toil A*L*O*N*E .

Affectionately,
George Pulver.

P. S. Please say hello to your Father and Mother.

---

*"Watch the grip of your left hand, that the knuckles face the target in the address,
and not the earth."— George Pulver*

I had a chance to return home for a longer stay if I got my studies in order. That seemed well worth it considering Mr. Pulver's recent health. A bout of poor putting on my part also seemed to perk him up. He wrote this — a list of considerations when one is trying to get back to hitting consistently good putts.

Grip tension, foot alignment, the path of the takeaway, aiming the club face properly, the way the left hand grips the club, keeping the club low to the ground on the backstroke, looking for patterns of misses, and even changing putters for a bit to reset your eyes, feel, and mental approach.

The list may seem long, but every point he makes is based on fact and pattern (where am I consistently missing it?) and the fundamentals necessary to create a consistent strike on the ball. Consistent strikes lead to consistent speed, which makes reading and feeling greens easier. And above all, speed dictates line. Let's say that again — speed dictates line.

How do we get consistent speed? Good fundamentals, plus solid and consistent strikes on the ball. All of this is a big, completely interconnected circle. When I was at my best, I could feel the strike in my hands before I ever settled in over a putt. I could feel the speed and the read become a direct byproduct of that; it was all linked together.

Due to his health, Mr. Pulver would not be able to attend the Albany awards dinner, but he was to be a part of the night nonetheless as I dedicated the honor to him. He may have believed I achieved as much as I did on my own, but none of it would have been possible without his guidance, education, patience, discipline, mentorship, and firm but kind manner.

Mr. Pulver's reaction to the award dedication was exactly as I expected; he said I minimized and understated my contribution.

News — Wednesday Afternoon, February 13, 1985 — 1B

Pepper's award goes elsewhere

Wilton golfer dedicates prize to her tutor

By TIM WILKIN
Assistant Sports Editor

Dottie Pepper's golfing career changed the day she met George Pulver.

In 1981, Pepper was a 15-year-old school girl who was on the verge of becoming the best female duffer the area has seen in the last 20 years.

And it was Pulver who brought it out.

Four years later, Pepper finds herself as a member of the Furman University women's golf team, and she still credits the 87-year-old Pulver as the driving force behind her success.

Last night, Pepper was honored as the top female collegiate athlete at the Fourth Annual Empire State Sports Award Dinner. It's the second time around for Pepper, who won it in the scholastic category two years ago.

But this one isn't hers — she's dedicating it to Pulver.

"Without him I wouldn't even be

Pepper: Wins award

close to where I am today," Pepper said. "He taught me the fundamentals of the game. Maybe the most important thing he taught me was how to handle the pressure of golf. I'm going to dedicate that award to him but I don't know if he'll take it.

"He made me appreciate the game more," she said. "This game is his life and he's just taught me so much."

Pulver, who was head pro at McGre-

gor Links Country Club for 40 years, taught her well. Last year, Pepper had the best score for an amateur at the prestigious U.S. Women's Open. She also finished fifth in the National Collegiate Women's Golf Championships and won the Duke Spring Invitational.

According to Pepper, it would have been almost impossible if not for the tutelage she received from Pulver.

"He taught me how to win and how to think my way around the golf course," she said. "He's still helping me. I talk to him all the time and we write letters back and forth while I'm at school. He's without a doubt the best teacher I could have ever had."

Pepper had a good fall season at Furman, except for an injury. She played in four tournaments: she won the Memphis Women's Intercollegiate; was second at the Alabama Seascape Invitational; and tied for third at Florida State's Lady Seminole Invitational. She withdrew at Miami's Pat Bradley

Invitational because of torn ligaments in her left ankle, an injury that occurred while she was playing racquetball a few days prior to the tourney.

She tried to play at Miami with a cast on her foot, but she couldn't continue.

Pepper's mended now and she's ready for the spring season, which begins March 1 with the Lady Spartan Invitational in Montery, Calif.

Now that she's an established golfer on the collegiate scene (she's been ranked nationally as high as fourth), Pepper prepering to join professional tour, but she'll have to wait two years. Her education comes first.

"I know that (going pro) is something I really want to do," she said. "I'm excited about it, but I'm going to stay in school and graduate. My parents would kick me out of the house if I didn't."

Other area athletes won awards last night:

Please see AWARD, Page 4B

A newspaper clipping from the Saratogian.

Miss Dottie Pepper
196 Correll Road
Glenwood NY 12831

Dottie:

Your news release was gret, but I fear you minimized and understated your own contribution. It was you who had agonized, worried and toiled. From our first meeting at therange , I was amazed at your ~~swing~~ skill, determination. You were certainly the most promising pupil I ever worked with.

OVER
P.S. to the very end. keep trying, and refused to be deterred bay set backs. Pleasee accept ax slight method changes in which, your confidence improves.

Well I remember the slashing flat swing of Hogan. The tightness of modern design for him to change to a more upright swing -- TOO MANY DUCK HOOKS. Also Jack Nichlaus comes to mind. His upright swing had to be flattened-- to a plane of his height i- HE WAS LOSING DISTANCE .

The main thing, undiminished determination to continue to keep trying, to the very end. At your point in time the mental factors, and the Will-To-Win must come first.

You owe me nothing. I shall remember forever you superb turn, steady head, unyielding left arm, a great forward thrust of your body as you start down, and priceless rythm. The trophy must go to the winner and remain with the winner.

Please pass along a word of cheer to your father and Mother. Anytime your feel you may need help please call on me or write me.

Sincerely yours

George J. Pulver.

P. S. Good luck on your Spring games.

This undated letter may look like a mess to most, but to me it showed how hard Mr. Pulver was fighting though his physical illness while still remaining so engaged mentally.

His pattern of continually stressing the importance of determination, finding one's own way with only slight method changes, and again illustrating his beliefs through professional examples, was completely intact.

March was, as usual, the time to start putting the summer schedule together, but our team traveled to compete over spring break for the first time. Minimizing the number of classroom days lost was a big deal at Furman, where many professors had individual attendance policies in addition to the university's own strict freshman policy. No days were lost if you played on breaks, so off we went to the Patty Sheehan Invitational at Fort Ord and Pebble Beach, California, and then to the University of Texas event on the way back to the East Coast.

The Furman golf team at Pebble Beach. Dottie is at far left.

As a broadcaster, I have covered events at Pebble Beach for nearly 20 years but I will never forget being there for the first time during that event. Thirty-six holes were played up the road at the Bayonet Course at Fort Ord and the final round at Pebble Beach. Mr. Pulver had told me about the history there, but to this day, it is the only competitive round I ever played where I took pictures. I still have them all.

Toward the end of spring break, I updated Mr. Pulver on my performance, my studies, and tournaments ahead.

AUSTIN HILTON INN
At Highland Mall

3-8-85

Dear Mr. Pulver,

Hi! How are you feeling? I hope you're continuing to improve. It won't be long before the good weather will be back and I'm sure that will help.

Today was the first day of the tournament here in Austin. Our team is in 2nd place, 4 behind Tulsa University. I had a very disappointing 77 (5 over). I was only 2 over through 16 holes and made a triple on 17. The big numbers seem to hit me once every round because I lose my concentration. I concentrate very well for 14-15 holes and then seem to let down and get unsettled. Do you have any suggestions to help me out of this? I finished in a tie for 7th last week in California, but the big numbers during the round (1 hole each round) kept me from winning it all. I feel like I'm right on the verge of breaking loose and playing some fantastic golf, but I just can't seem to break the barrier.

We're heading back to school Sunday night and school starts again Tuesday morning. We've been on spring break for the last two weeks and it has allowed us to play 2 big tournaments without missing any classes. The third round of last week's tournament was played at Pebble Beach. What an experience that was! It has to be the finest designed course I've ever played, not to mention its beauty. When I paced off the yardages last Saturday at sunset, I took some beautiful pictures. I'll have to show you them when I come home. I had the strangest feeling walking down #18 knowing all the history that has been made there.

Earlier tonight I spoke to my father. My grades from

IH 35 at Highland Mall   Austin, Texas 78752   512/451-5757

the winter term had come in the mail. I made a B+ and an A. That pulls my overall G.P.A. up to 3.02. This coming term I'm scheduled to take 4 classes: "Religion in America," "Exercise Physiology," "Softball," and "China & Communism." Two of them are standard university requirements and the other two are courses in my major.

Well- I've got some good news. I've been invited to the LPGA Moss Creek Invitational at Hilton Head Island, S.C. May 2-5. Only 90 professionals and 10 amateurs were invited to play. It's the equivalent of the Masters. Moss Creek is supposed to be an excellent and difficult golf course so, as you can probably tell, I'm very excited about it. I also got an invitation to the Nabisco Dinah Shore, but declined it because of the expense, the convenience of the Moss Creek tournament being just 4 1/2 hours from school, and the date conflicting with my defense of my title at Duke that same weekend. Maybe I'll get another invitation and be able to go next year.

Well, it's getting late and I really should get some rest for tomorrow's round. Please give my best to Madelyn, Jean, and George along with their families. Take care of yourself- I'll see you in a few weeks! ☺
Hope to hear from you soon.

All my love,
Dottie

My mention of getting big numbers on the scorecard and not being able to hold my concentration over the last couple of events certainly didn't cause him any alarm. In fact, he seemed to almost brush it aside in his response of March 14, again using Bobby Jones as an example of a player who had come so close, so often, only to be repeatedly turned back. Having Mr. Pulver be able to identify with players and history was invaluable to me and made me feel like I wasn't the only one to have to clear these seemingly large speed bumps.

The summer schedule did begin to take on a new look after the 1984 U.S. Women's Open, with invitations to two events on the LPGA schedule, the Nabisco Dinah Shore in April and the Moss Creek Invitational in May. What did not take on a new look was the economics of playing competitive golf away from school. Traveling to Southern California, major championship or not, was simply not in the budget. Writing the letter to decline the invitation tore me up but there was no other option. Moss Creek was a drive trip from school with an offer of private housing. Moss Creek turned out to be a wonderful experience, but having to pass on the Dinah invitation stung.

Dottie's invitation to the 1985 Dinah Shore event. She had to decline

I can promise you having to turn down the invitation to the Dinah as an amateur made my two victories there as a professional even more special. The tournament was also important because in 1988, it would be my first top-10 finish in a major, capping a two-week run where I made enough money to stay on tour for the entire season and ensure my playing privileges for the next year.

Mr. Pulver continued to stress the importance of solid fundamentals in putting and offered a suggestion for a drill — the three-foot drill — that I often used. It centered on holing three putts from around a practice hole, not standing in one place, hitting the same putt time after time. There is time for that monotony if the mechanics of the stroke are a problem, but this was about holing putts — hearing and seeing them go in without an early peek. But it was also hitting putts that were not identical to each other. If one can be perfect on putts from three feet and in, the rest of the game becomes immeasurably freer, all the way from chipping and pitching, bunker play, approach shots, and even driving the golf ball.

There was a touch of sadness toward the end of his letter, though, that got to me. It was more and more painful to use his hands, and the health issues of the winter had clearly taken a toll on his spirit.

"Your long game has reached such excellence, from now on you must master now and then those lightning greens. The most important thing in my judgement is to keep your eye on the backside of the ball until it is dispatched." — George Pulver

Friday, 14 of March 1985

Dottie:

Keep trying! I predict that big numbers at the end of your round shall vanish.

Well I recall the great Bobby Jones for eight tantalizing years was the best striker of a golf ball in all the world. Again and again when it appeared that he had a tournamenti in the bag, he throws in a bad round. About the time Jones and his followers had about given up on he becomig a champion, the tide turned. and he won eight championships around the world. and indeed became the greatest hitter of a ball in the world.

I enclose a cut from a recent P. G. A. magazine showing a dejected Toski. Bob Toski has stayed in many championships, and was never known to quit. He is a cool and strong finisher, with vast competitive experience. He had round of 70- 73-74, and finished with an inglorious 80. That 80 near the finishe of his last round did him in. andc cost him about $7000 in prize money. The trap-shot displayed was sculled across the green.

I would like to talked to you on chips and short putts. Your long game has reac such excellence, from now on you must master now and then those lightning greens. The most important thing in my judgement is to keep your eye on the backside of the ball until it is dispatched. This will aid in not swaying. On a fast green after a few misses, a momentary look up will invite disaster. And the worst part, the player will discover his errancy too late. In going to a course, I would suggest that you drop four balls around a hole on the putting clock, and keep trying to hole them out. Three foot putts are the one to practice. Try holing them out, with a firm grip relaxed arms and shoulders, using a slow backswing.If you find that agin and again you miss slightly to the right or left check your foot line. it may help to hae it parallel withthe hole, but it does not hae to be. Your eyes may be slightly off. And the center of the equation, has to be. your confidence—which means concentration which you have found out. The shot which counts is the one coming up.

Finally, a straight foot line at the hole, helps, but many great putters go from a minutely closed stance or open stance, or any position which promotes comfidence. By trial and error find your own most successful way, and settle on it.

Dottie, I have arthritis in my finger, and it is difficult for me to type In fact this pastwinter, has been the most provocative in my life time.

Sincerely,

Your Mother stopped by a few days ago, and we enjoyed her company. Your felicitations in the mentioning of my children was indeed most kind. I LIKE YOUR ACADEMICS AND YOUR COUR COURSE SELECTIONS.

Mr. Pulver's chief mentor, Seymour Dunn, came to this country from Scotland for the first time in 1894, traveling with his father, the golf course architect Tom Dunn, to the New York area. Seymour would settle in the United States in 1907 but it is his family's lineage back to the very beginnings of the game at Leith Links in Scotland and Blackheath in London that left an indelible mark on Mr. Pulver. They were golf professionals with skill sets that included club making, teaching, and course design, as well as being champion golfers. Mr. Pulver followed them in developing those same varied skills, and I was beyond blessed to have someone like him to continue to learn from.

Mr. Pulver references his Scottish connections in this letter.

The Seymour Dunn golf shop in Lake Placid, New York. Dunn opened his first assembly line for golf clubs in 1910.
Photo courtesy of the Lake Placid Historical Society

April 5, 1185

Dottie:

This is no letter -- I just wanted to say hello!

For the first ten years of my golf experience I worked
with Scotch Pro.s and club makers, directly from Scotland

The photo which no doub you have seen, is Ben Crenshaw
addressing a putt.   This is the precise position that
my early Scotch tutors assumed when addressing a Drive.

Crenshaw, starting away in photo #2, no early wrist action,
slow back, arm amd club in one line, but not stiff or tense/
He returns to his address position at impact. But as important
as this is, the thing that makes Crenshaw a fine putter, is his
phlosophy, his relaxed manner. Whether he is going for the
Masters, or a round with a hustler, he does not tighten-up

On the other hand, lets look at, one who picks up the slub
it seems to me with the right hand, but he stays loose
and at the top he is in a superb position. with the left arm
in line with the ball. He is Fuzzy Zoeller. Fuzzy is a strong
man with a complete swing, big hands, and a wonderful temperment for goolf.

Now Pat Bradley. She is short, takes the club inside too soon
moves the ball from Right to Left, to get added distance. But
in my view, her face in the news photo, show determination, concentration, that is why she is near the top for the past 10 years.

I am trying to say, it takes years of hard work, and toil,
to get in top-flight competion, but to be a champion, you need
all of this, a delicate touch around the greens, and ability
under fire to produce. I feel that I havesome ability to mechanically
teach but I must confess, that I never played enought or worked
on my game, nor had the time with my numerous chores. The old Scotch
professionals, got ready for the Open with a few days away from
their clubs. In fact, many years ago, I had a course in Nassau, B W. I.
Jock and I had another one down the road, We were in the same hotel,
and I played often with him. Jock has a fast flat swing, uswing
a left shoulder turn way beyond the back of the ball. H was a short
iron player. bit he could move the ball with the moderns off the tee.

A modern player must have length, luck, and mental fortitude.

Please say hello to your Father and Mother, Personally, I have
had a tough winter , with five or six saw-bones trying to find
my troubles physically.

Keep trying. You are about to get out in front. Remember Bobbie
Jones one of the great players of all time, yet he thru away
seven National titlees by errant concentration on many of the
finishing holes. The next eight years h swept the world, winning
eight National Tournaments.

From the beginning of our relationship, Mr. Pulver forbid me from reading the instruction articles in golf magazines, instead encouraging me to focus on the people, the places, the tournaments, and the mental makeup of champions, leaving the mechanics to his teaching, not someone else's. If he saw an article of particular value, he would cut it out and add it to his collection. If he felt it applied to me, it would end up in my mailbox.

I was gifted that collection of articles in 2010 by George Jr. The forbidden reading was, and still is, in a ragged folder. They date from mid-1966 to mid-1985, most underlined with Mr. Pulver's commentary scratched in the margins. It was in this forbidden folder that I discovered that I wasn't the only one accumulating a collection of letters. He was also keeping every letter I wrote to him.

He continued to help me find the players I could identify with and the parts of their games that would help me most, whether it be Ben Crenshaw's relaxed setup over the putter, Fuzzy Zoeller's takeaway, or Pat Bradley's determination and concentration. He believed champions were a total package that ultimately could produce when it mattered most. As usual, he summed it up concisely in just one line: "A modern player must have length, luck, and mental fortitude." He believed a champion's greatest strength is having no glaring weakness. That was always my goal; seldom achieved but always the goal.

Pat Bradley at the 1996 Solheim Cup. Photo courtesy of Elizabeth Opalenik

With his hands swollen by arthritis, he began to share his thoughts through articles even more frequently. It hurt less than typing and he could highlight the things he felt were most important in a short note or in the margins of the articles. His pursuit of golf knowledge had not waned a bit, it was just getting tougher to hammer out those thoughts on his typewriter's bulky keys.

Monday, April 29, 1985

MISS DOTTIE PEPPER
Box 196,
Furman University Box 27934
Greenville, N. C.

Dottie:

Your mother has been good enought to keep me informed of your progress.
You have done everything as well as could be expected. Hang, in there!

I am taking the liberty of enclosing several articles that may catch
your interest. The great players of the world have gone through just
what you are enduring. The few that did not had the unique temperment
such as perhaps a Watson or a Zoeller. And already many of the great men
players are seeking the Seniour events, and letting the young Turks take
over.

Please do not bother to reply. Your turn shall come.!

George J,

The four rounds at the Moss Creek Invitational were extremely positive, reinforcing that I was on the track to turn pro in two years. But I had a big concern — one that made me sound like today's players: I needed to hit the ball farther!

Part of the problem was certainly equipment. I still couldn't afford the equipment that was hottest at the time. But another part was that at age 19, I was still developing the muscle mass and body control that the professionals I competed against already had. My tool box was still being filled, and I was impatient. Heck, I still can't spell the word "patient" 35-plus years later.

MAY 7

Dear Mr. Pulver,

Hi! Thank you for all of your letters and articles. My game seems to be coming along well. I feel good about my play at Moss Creek this past week and feel confident that in 2 years I will be ready to face up to the challenge on a regular basis. My frame of mind is really good and I'm looking forward to the NCAA Championship in 2 weeks.

My main concern after a week with the pros is my lack of distance off the tee. I don't see any way I can consistently spot people 20-40 yards and beat them. My iron play is just slightly shorter than theirs, which I feel will be taken care of through better timing and strength in the next 2 years, but my driving definitely has me concerned. A metal-headed driver seems to be the only answer. I'm a bit hesitant about putting a graphite shaft with the metal head because my timing seems to be thrown off, but I definitely need more distance if I'm going to make a living off this game. If you have any suggestions about which model of driver and type of shaft I should get, please let me know.

I hope all is going well up there for you. I understand that the golf courses really need some rain. We could use some rain here, too; it was a very dry winter.

I think of you often and am looking forward to working with you again in about a month.

Hope to hear from you soon.
Love,
Dottie

Mr. Pulver, of course, put it in perspective, asking how my length was in comparison to my college peers, not the LPGA professionals. It was a fair and accurate question. He also reinforced that while I was seeking length, I shouldn't ignore my short game, something that so often happens as players focus on gaining distance or making a wholesale swing change. The short game will always help make up for mistakes in the long game. The long game may even be freed up when the player knows he or she has a well-tended short game in her back pocket.

Dear Dottie: Sunday May 12, 1985

Your recent letterr encourages me. Your frame of mind eloquently speaks to your thinking.

You report lack of distance --in an ordinary way this surprises me. Of course, the girls are bigger, are playing more, and in the class your competitions are not the best in this broad land, but throughout the world.

First, look at your timimg. I am saying when you flush one, it should feel soldid and you should be on your feet. Your hope in a steel headed graphyte driver, may be valid. A help may be to use your wrist action in yodur up-swing as late as you can--this gill increase your left shoulder turn, and perhaps slightly flatten the plane of your swing.

I have such a club as you describe --About C-8 S.W. Total weight 13 ounces, Length 43 inches, shaft regular men's graphyte. It must be in your range. I ask, how is your length against that of the college girls you play with, not the top-Pros in the world.

Good luck, and keep trying. Keep an effort to achieve putting and chipping skills this is the central idea at this time.

Sincerely

Both the team and I had a very strong spring and went into the NCAA Championship at New Seabury, Massachusetts, with justifiably high expectations. Personally, it was a chance for redemption after closing out the '84 championship with a humiliating and costly four-putt. But we also had one of the best teams in the country. It would be tougher for us, but we knew that even before the championship dates were announced.

We had not yet taken final exams and would be studying for them through nationals, but we were used to packing the books for tournaments and studying at night, in vans, and on planes. This championship was an even bigger deal for me, because New Seabury was just over three hours from home, and my family would see me play a college event for the first time.

My four-part game plan held solid for the first three rounds: no need to be a hero, eliminate mistakes and big numbers, hang tough if a bad patch comes along, and par fives aren't worth the risk of going for them in two shots. I was one shot off the lead, and the team was right in it, too, after a championship low score of 294 on Day Three.

The plan was to do exactly the same for the final round. It was then that I learned how it can be equally damaging to be reckless with your course management and so inflexible and conservative that you cannot let yourself make a necessary play. I hit an enormous tee shot at the par-five first hole, leaving about 200 yards to the hole. No water to negotiate, no other hazards worth worrying about. I had told myself I wasn't going to deviate from the plan, so I laid up — with a pitching wedge — and made a sloppy bogey. That inflexibly timid play set the tone for the entire day. I was rattled and had anything but the plodding "hang in there" mentality that Mr. Pulver had worked so hard to carve and polish.

Not only did I cost myself the individual title, my score of 79 kept our team off the podium for the second straight year, missing a third-place finish by a shot. It was a brutal day, reinforcing that I still had a lot to learn, including being able to change the game plan's gears when situations like I had at the first hole present themselves. In military terms, it is like saying "no plan survives contact with the enemy." You have to be confident enough in your preparation and aware enough of your circumstances to call that audible.

Dottie and her grandfather "Pa" at the 1985 NCAA Championship at New Seabury.
He would later float Dottie a $5,000 loan that got her started on her LPGA Tour journey.

For instance, Collin Morikawa likely would not be the 2020 PGA Champion if he hadn't decided to give himself well-considered permission to break from his week-long game plan to lay up at the drivable 16th hole in the final round. As late as the final practice round, Collin had been vocal and decisive in saying that he would not be attempting to go for the green from the tee, instead laying up to play to his superb wedge game. But the conditions and circumstances changed. He hit the driver inside 10 feet from hole that last day, made the eagle putt and ultimately won the championship. Decisions such as these are known as "flexible confidence" in my world today. Mr. Pulver would have loved that play as preparation met circumstance and confidence.

I called Mr. Pulver after the final round meltdown and, as usual, he used it to look at the long view. He encouraged me to take my time on this journey and work on better management, something that would come with more experience and patience (there is that dreadful word again!) He knew I needed a quick reset with finals beginning as soon as we got back to school. A full summer tournament schedule was also ahead with some of the best events in women's golf coming to the Northeast again.

He was having a run of better days with the spring turning to summer, but in his own way summed up his condition, saying "I feel okay, but my age is here."

May 26, 1985

Dear Dottie:

I enclose some local clippings, no doubt you already have them.

D'ont try to run too fast. You have done wonderfully. When they day come that your scoring might be a few shots improved, it will be in management.

Of the thousands of girls, from all over the land, trying to reach the top, for two years in a row you have led the amateurs. The difference in my view between the pros and top-amateurs is slight, and mostly in management. Be patient--I can understand your pressure, but the top shall be reached with lurches, and time.

No reply--I shall see you when you return. Try to also keep up in your school work. I feel okey, but the age is here. Say hello to your father and mother.

Sincerely,

June 19, 1985

Dottie:

It was indeed apleasure to see you hit the ball so well.

Now golf--Your idea of line up is excellent. On the big shots, shoulder and ball line in the same paralel, but about 20 iches apart because of the hang of your arms.

Your swing is the modern swing completely, but be sure that you go back on your line, or a wild shot to the right may occur, or a quick turn over of your wrists (hook)

Getting back to getting natural, is only confidence during a con- test. You have attacked millions of golf balls, you recall how you felt on the perfect shots.

Therefore, try finding your most natural position, and should too many shots go astray --have someone look at your swing. I suspect that already your swing has jelled where it belong, under pressure you must try to feel your self.

In the old days most of the champion golfers swing flat, except, Vardon he bent his left arm at the top, and by some miracle restored it coming down. In our modern era, Nicholas comes to mind with an extreme upright swing. It is nice to bring the ball in from left to right, but much strength has to be lost. Lets keep trying to move the ball a little to the left, because of the long courses, and distance factor.

In practice try to make four or five shots in a row, with the same feel, then move to another club up. And observe the bodies of your opponents. Some are much heavier than you are, and perhaps stronger. In my view you have a swing that fits your body.

I observed that you squared your club face nicely at the address, and kept it square to the ball. Most important, and aids in your swing plane, and obviates a right hand turn-over as the ball is hit.

Good luck, and be patient.

Say hello to your mother and father.

Sincerely

"In practice, try to make four or five shots in a row, with the same feel, then move to another club up. And observe the bodies of your opponents. … In my view, you have a swing that fits your body." — George Pulver

We planned to resume working together as soon as I got back from the Eastern Amateur. We discussed no big changes in our routine, but he did plant the seed that I would need a different set of eyes — not his — to look at my golf swing. His eyesight was failing. He continued to reiterate the fundamentals of the setup, being in a natural position at address, and maintaining a swing that fits your body — evergreen checkpoints that still apply to today's teachers and students.

Mr. Pulver's practice advice in this letter is one of my favorites and one that I used, and even expanded a bit, during my playing career. He liked a practice session to have some form, direction, and purpose — not to have a player be on the range beating balls for the sake of just beating balls. Being a believer in being able to feel the shots, he liked me to go through the bag with every club, hitting four or five in a row with the same pre-shot routine, the same feel. It kept practice positive, varied, and interesting. Later, I would expand this to 10 shots per club, going up the bag from wedges to driver and then back down again to the short clubs.

Four days later, everything Mr. Pulver and I had been working on physically — as well as some time spent with the sports psychologist, Dr. Ken Ravizza — came together in winning the Albany-Colonie Open on the Futures (now Symetra) Tour. I became the first amateur in history to win on that professional tour. With no leaderboards around the course, I holed a 10-foot putt for par on the final hole for a one-shot win, but I thought the putt was for a three-way tie and a playoff. My sister, Jackie, caddied for me — she thought it was for a tie, too! Winning that tournament, in that manner, just 25 miles from home was most definitely a "hang in there" moment. Another reinforcement that we were on the right track.

Pepper becomes first amateur to win Futures

By Tim Wilkin
Staff writer

COLONIE — In terms of money, she didn't win a dime. But Dottie Pepper won a million dollars worth of respect from her golfing peers Sunday.

Pepper, the 19-year-old golfing whiz from Wilton, captured the $15,000 Futures Golf Tournament at the 6,100-yard Town of Colonie Golf Course.

"I think it's just great that an amateur could come in and win this,"

> *This is just the greatest. It ranks up there as one of the biggest thrills of my career.*
>
> **— Dottie Pepper**

said 24-year-old Janice Gibson, who won first place prize money after winning a one-hole playoff from Betsy Barrett. "I wish I was as good a player as she is when I was an amateur. She has the potential to be a great golfer; she's already an excellent one."

"I couldn't be happier for her," said Chatham's Eloise Trainor, president of the Futures Tour. "It gives a lot of credit to the college golf programs around the country."

Pepper, who just completed her sophomore year at Furman University, shot a 1-under-par 71 Sunday, giving her a 2-over total of 218 and the title. It was the first time an amateur had ever won on the Futures Tour, which is made up of women aspiring to one day

make it to the Ladies Professional Golf Association Tour.

Because of her amateur status, Pepper wasn't able to take home the first-prize purse of $2,250. That went to Gibson of Stillwater, Okla., after she sank a 15-foot putt on the first hole of a sudden death playoff. Barrett, of Campbell, Calif., took third place and the second money prize of $1,750. Jody Rosenthal of Edina, Minn., the 1984 British Amateur champion, finished fourth in her professional debut with a 220 and earned $1,350.

The suspense was over long before the playoff. Most of the people in attendance Sunday were there to see Pepper. And they went home happy.

Pepper clinched the title on the 395-yard, par-4 18th hole — a hole she had bogeyed the first two days of the tourney.

By that time, her gallery had grown to more than 300 people — more than half the people in attendance — and Pepper sank a 10-foot putt for par.

At first she thought she was tied with Gibson. After she was set straight, it was celebration time.

"This is just the greatest," Pepper said. "It ranks up there as one of the biggest thrills of my career."

Her short career has been highlighted by being the low amateur at the Women's U.S. Open last year and also taking second place at the NCAA Women's Championships last month.

Pepper started the day tied for the lead with Barrett at 147. She shot a 1-under-par 35 on the front nine, thanks to a pair of birdies on the sixth and seventh holes. Barrett had a 36 on the front and Gibson a 35.

After Pepper bogeyed the 10th hole, she was tied for the lead with Barrett but Gibson passed them both with a birdie on the 11th hole.

Pepper's title run started on the 16th hole, a 485-yard, par 5.

Gibson, playing ahead of Pepper,

See **PEPPER** / C-6

Top finishers' cards: (Final round)

Hole	1	2	3	4	5	6	7	8	9	
Par Out	4	5	4	3	5	4	4	3	4	36
Pepper	5	5	4	3	5	3	3	3	4	35
Gibson	4	5	3	3	4	4	5	3	4	35
Barrett	5	5	3	3	4	4	4	3	5	36

Hole	10	11	12	13	14	15	16	17	18	
Par In	4	5	4	3	4	4	5	3	4	36-72-216
Pepper	5	5	4	3	4	4	4	3		36-71-218
Gibson	4	4	4	3	4	5	6	2	4	36-72-219
Barrett	4	5	4	3	4	4	5	3	4	36-72-219

Janice Gibson won a one-hole playoff with Barrett for first-prize money.

FUTURE IS NOW — Although she didn't take home any money because of her amateur status, Wilton's Dottie Pepper was the crowd favorite, attracting a gallery of more than 300 fans.

Times Union photo by Fred McKinney

A clipping from the Albany Times-Union.

DOTTIE: Saturday July 10th, 1985

More than 50 years I have been enthralled with the teaching of
of golf. I have found that the profoundest of Jones, surpasses
that of any writers. There are so many truths, found in this book,
that I feel the urge to leave it in your box. to explore.

In my opionion, your swing cannot be improved, but perhaps your concentrat
can.   Recently, the only error I could discern--you may start back a little
fast, neglect to get the left side around, then from your upright
swing come down from the outside, and get a duck hook, or a weak
shot to the right.
Too much is expected of you. Stay loose in the shoulders and get the
right hip turning as you go back, so the large muscles of the body
can provide the power, and proper swing plane. An old caddie may not
be able to break 90 but caddying again and again over the same turf
he has gained an intuitive insight of the subtle breaks.

You have a glorious way of attacking a golf ball--do not change.
Good luck, and as sure as night follows day, your time shall come
to lead the pack.
No   reply please, but return Jones's Golf Book at your leisure.
I am stumbling, in my health. but I shall carry on .
Say hello to your Father and Mother.

Sincerely

GJB.

Ken Ravizza had made the trip from Cal-State Fullerton to Furman earlier in the year, lecturing within the HPE Department but also doing some more detailed work with our golf team. Mr. Pulver knew I needed to hear about the mental part of the game from someone other than him and encouraged my work with Ken. I went through some bad bouts of visualization from time to time; because I was losing focus, I didn't have a lot of fun playing and practicing. It's a pretty darn normal thing to fight, but having Mr. Pulver recognize that someone else could help me in a way he couldn't spoke to his selfless nature and his desire for me to be as good as I could be.

In early July, Mr. Pulver sent me another reading assignment, *The Bobby Jones Story*. Among the many underlined and dog-eared pages is one he obviously thought to be of particular importance because it dealt with concentration. Jones believed that it was a mistake and nearly impossible for him to concentrate straight through an entire round. Jones liked to find a bit of relief from the tension of a tournament round and then snap back into concentration as needed. Mr. Pulver and Ken Ravizza never spoke but their shared belief in this method was uncanny and one I believe to be so valuable. When it was time to execute under pressure, Ken likened that moment to a picture clicking into sharper focus, one frame at a time. Leave it to Mr. Pulver to find just the perfect piece of literature to support this with a player he so revered, Bobby Jones, as the example.

Mr. Pulver would again allude to his health being a challenge but he continued to work with me throughout what would be a solid summer, making the cut at the U.S. Women's Open again, reaching the third round of the U.S. Women's Amateur, and winning a couple of the local women's team events as well. I'd found a terrific partner in Sheila Vergith, one of my most enthusiastic supporters while

The Bobby Jones Story

stood on the last tee at Scioto, with a 480-yard hole on which to get a birdie four to go ahead of Joe Turnesa?" I asked. Bobby grinned reflectively. "I thought I'd sock this one," he replied. "But that was before I swung. I didn't think of anything consciously while I was swinging."

Well, he socked it 310 yards, with the wind against him. And he got home with a spared mashie iron second, and got the birdie four, and won the championship. This indicates it pays not to think – while swinging.

"There's another thing," said Bobby. "I try never to force a club any more. Rather than hit hard with a mashie, I take a number four iron. It seems I can keep the 'feel' of that left hand better, that way."

About the nerve strain in tournament play.

"There are two kinds of golf," said Bobby seriously. "There is golf – and tournament golf. And they are not at all alike, inside. I have found that out from experience, much of it bitter. I'm more nervous before medal competition than match. In a match you have a single human opponent, who may make some mistakes. In medal play you are up against Old Man Par, who never gets down in one putt and never takes three. The first round of an open championship always causes me the most suffering. It's worse than the last, oddly enough. You see, in starting, I don't know how I'm going to be hitting my shots the first few holes. The start at Scioto was torture, because I had played wretchedly in practice and was uncertain if I could hit the ball decently. I do not think nervousness hurts my game. The more nervous I am, the better I play, usually. I suppose it means being keyed up. Some of the sloppiest rounds I have played I was not nervous at all. As to the strain, I don't seem to be conscious of it during a round. Afterward – well, I know something has been done to me. I sort of collapsed at Columbus after getting back to the hotel. I was all in."

· 200 ·

SEPT. 30, 1985

DEAR MR. PULVER —

Hi! HOW ARE YOU DOING? THINGS ARE GOING PRETTY WELL HERE. I GOT OFF TO A REAL ROUGH START WITH MY SCHOOLWORK, BUT IT SEEMS TO BE GETTING A LITTLE BETTER NOW. I'M TAKING MATH, SPANISH AND MUSIC — — NOT THE EASIEST COMBINATION WHEN I'M MISSING SO MUCH FOR GOLF TOURNAMENTS. I'VE ENCLOSED OUR NEW PROGRAM FOR YOU — THOUGHT YOU MIGHT LIKE IT.

WE JUST GOT BACK FROM OHIO STATE UNIV. LAST NIGHT. THE TEAM FINISHED 3RD AND I FINISHED 15TH WITH 75-79-78. I HAD VERY STRONG ROUNDS GOING ALL 3 DAYS AND LET IT GET AWAY FROM ME EACH TIME. I DON'T KNOW WHY IT HAPPENED, BUT IT DID. I PLAYED PRETTY WELL AT FLORIDA STATE LAST WEEK AND FINISHED 4TH WITH 74-76-71. I'M STRIKING THE BALL WELL, BUT I'M NOT SCORING THE WAY I SHOULD. FRIDAY WE'RE LEAVING AGAIN FOR MEMPHIS STATE — — A BORING 10 HOUR DRIVE FROM HERE.

THE WEATHER HAS BEEN FANTASTIC — — HIGH 70'S TO MID 80'S EVERY DAY. I HAVE TO SPEND SOME TIME ON THE BOOKS THIS AFTERNOON, BUT TOMORROW I PLAN ON PRACTICING ALL AFTERNOON. THE ONLY REAL THING I'M HAVING TROUBLE WITH ARE MY LAG PUTS OVER 30 FEET — — I'M CONSTANTLY LEAVING THEM 5-8 FEET SHORT, HITTING THEM THIN AND THEY'RE BOUNCING OFF THE CLUB FACE REALLY BADLY. I DON'T KNOW WHAT I'M DOING WRONG WITH THEM.

WELL, I NEED TO GO TO MY SPANISH CLASS NOW. HOPE YOU'RE FEELING BETTER AND I LOOK FORWARD TO HEARING FROM YOU SOON.

PLEASE GIVE MY BEST TO YOUR FAMILY.

ALL MY LOVE,
Dottie

coming up through the ranks of the Capital District golf scene. I was still checking those important "Pulver boxes" with local and regional competitions and having fun doing it with Sheila.

The biggest change with Mr. Pulver as the summer of 1985 wore on was that he would rely heavily on a lawn chair to sit in while we worked on the range. He had it with him occasionally the previous summer, but now it was a constant. His physical strength was fading, but his mind was ever sharp and his hearing — well, I still couldn't hit a less-than-perfect shot without him noticing it instantly.

Returning to school knowing that Mr. Pulver's health was such a challenge was not easy, but we continued to write. As usual I was sharing updates on tournaments, classes, and anything that was trending in my game. He was always equally interested in the academics and on-course results.

Mr. Pulver's letter of Oct. 5 would turn out to be his last typewritten letter to me but one that highlighted three key points, all centered on putting.

"I am delighted that you are striking the ball well – that is in the last analysis the thing. Don't be too fussy but try to discover the direction of grain growth, by the color of the growing grass. Many great putters say they take the club back with the left hand. I am less than certain that is so. In any event the right hand must carry the blade straight to the hole." — George Pulver

October 5 1985

My dear Dottie:

Your letter and Furman folder has made a day for me.   First of all,
I want to address you on putting. Putts that end up shrt and fall-off
can be traced to looking up just before contact. And fast greens,
and lag_ing putts will most surely promote this sort of thing. In my
view great putters do most of the stroking with the right hand, if they are
right-handed people.   After you have determine the spot on the ball which
you intend to strike --see that spot until the ball is on its way.   It
will take courage on fast greens, but try kepoing your eye on the ball,
til it is on its way.   Of course certain people have superior vision
and concentration but they are few in numbers.

In the olden days many of the putters were slightly lofted, to get the ball
over the 4/16"grass. Now in many championships, the cut of the grass has
been about 1/16" then they are rolled and slightly watered. Too much
emphasis has been placed on tough.

I am delighted that you are striking the ball well--that is in the last
analysis the thing.   Don't be too fussy but try to discover the direction
of grain growth, by the color of the growing grass. Many great putters
say they take the club back with the left hand. I am less than certains
that this is so.   In any event the right hand must carry the blade straight
to the hole.   A slightly opens stance seems to be the vogue.

Actually, I feel that you are trying so hard tension is taking over. I must
warn you that I am a louzy putter, so beware of this advice.

I approve your courses. One day you may need such courses.   Surely,
you would rather be on the course, but I am less than certain, that would
aid your putting but little.

This letter is less complete. but I am suffereing from a constantly hooked
Middle finger.   One day. I shall get back to you. Hangin there'. Geo

FURMAN UNIVERSITY

Dottie Pepper,
1985 NCAA Runnerup

F **LADY PALADIN GOLF 1985-86**

THE COACHES
Head Coach
Mic Potter

Mic Potter has established himself as one of the nation's top golf coaches in just three years at the helm of Furman University's women's program.

The 30-year-old native of Cortland, N.Y., has garnered three Top Ten finishes in the last three NCAA national championship tournaments. The Lady Paladins finished fourth in the NCAAs at Cape Cod, Massachusetts, in the spring of '85 after placing third and ninth the previous two seasons.

Potter came to Furman in February of 1978, taking over as the assistant golf professional at the university course. Since September of '79, he has served as the head pro at the 6,800-yard course, considered one of the best collegiate golf courses in the country.

Prior to coming to Furman, Potter was an assistant golf pro at Cortland Country Club in his hometown.

A 1977 graduate of Cortland State University, Potter earned his degree in physical education and was an outstanding athlete there. He lettered three years in soccer and once in golf while at Cortland, and prior to that had been a four-sport athlete at Cincinnatus Central School. Potter earned letters in golf, basketball, baseball and soccer and was a high school all-American in soccer.

Furman's head women's coach is known as a superb teacher of the game and his Lady Paladin schedule always includes some of the top collegiate competition in the nation.

Potter is married to the former Kim O'Branski of Ithaca, N.Y., and the couple has two children—Ryan, age three, and Corey, who will be two in October.

1984-85 STATISTICS
STROKE AVERAGES FOR TOP PLAYERS

	Tourneys	Rounds	Strokes	Avg
DOTTIE PEPPER	11	30	2283	76.1
SARA ANN TIMMS	11	32	2469	77.2
KATHY HART	11	31	2410	77.9
KRISTIN LOFYE	7	20	1594	79.7
KELLIE STENZEL	10	29	2342	80.8
MARGARET WILL	7	18	1478	81.7

LADY PALADIN GOLF 1984-1985 TEAM RESULTS

Tournament (Site)	FU Finish	Score	Low Individual (Finish, Score)
Lady Seminole Invitational (Tallahassee, FL)	2nd of 19	900	Dottie Pepper (T3rd, 219)
Carrier-Memphis Classic (Memphis, TN)	T2nd of 18	630	DOTTIE PEPPER (1ST, 151)
Alabama Seascape Invitational (Destin, FL)	1ST OF 17	605	Dottie Pepper (2nd, 146)
Pat Bradley Invitational (Miami, FL)	8th of 14	967	Sara Anne Timms (T10th, 234)
Patty Sheehan Invitational (Monterrey, CA)	8th of 11	963	Dottie Pepper (T7th, 232)
Betsy Rawls Invitational (Austin, TX)	5th of 18	915	Kathy Hart (6th, 223)
Lady Paladin Invitational (Greenville, SC)	1ST OF 23	924	Sara Anne Timms (2nd, 226)
Lady Gamecock Invitational (Columbia, SC)	4th of 14	932	Dottie Pepper (3rd, 225)
Duke Spring Invitational (Durham, NC)	1ST OF 16	924	SARA ANNE TIMMS (1ST, 227)*
Women's Southern Intercollegiate (Athens, GA)	4th of 16	928	Kathy Hart (T4th, 223)
NCAA Women's Championship (Cape Cod, MA)	4th of 18	1237	Dottie Pepper (2nd, 239)

*Timms defeated Dottie Pepper on the 1st hole of sudden death playoff

THE TRADITION
Furman in the National Championships

Year	Sanction	Site	Finish
1974	AIAW	San Diego, California	3rd
1975	AIAW	Tuscon, Arizona	5th
1976	**AIAW**	**East Lansing, Michigan**	**1st**
1977	AIAW	Honolulu, Hawaii	23rd
1978	AIAW	Gainesville, Florida	20th
1980	AIAW	Albuquerque, New Mexico	13th
1982		Columbus, Ohio	9th
1983	NCAA	Athens, Georgia	3rd
1984	NCAA	Tarpon Springs, Florida	3rd
1985	NCAA	Cape Cod, Massachusetts	4th

TEAM TOURNAMENT VICTORIES

Year Tournament	Year Tournament
1972 Lady Paladin Invitational	1978 Lady Tar Heel Invitational
1974 Lady Paladin Invitational	1983 Taylor Made-Memphis Classic
Women's Southern Intercoll.	Duke Spring Invitational
1975 Mary Baldwin Invitational	1984 Lady Paladin Invitational
Lady Paladin Invitational	Duke Spring Invitational
Randolph-Macon Invitational	Fall Creek Falls Classic
1976 Lady Gator Invitational	1985 Alabama Seascape Invitational
Peggy Kirk Bell Invitational	Lady Paladin Invitational
Michigan State Invitational	Duke Spring Invitational
AIAW Nat. Championships	

INDIVIDUAL TOURNAMENT VICTORIES

Year	Tournament	Player
1972	Lady Paladin Invitational	Beth Solomon
1974	Lady Paladin Invitational	Cindy Ferro
1975	Mary Baldwin Invitational	Cindy Ferro
	Lady Paladin Invitational	Betsy King
	Randolph-Macon Invitational	Beth Daniel
1976	Lady Gator Invitational	Betsy King
	Peggy Kirk Bell Invitational	Betsy King
	Michigan State Invitational	Betsy King
1977	Betsy Rawls Invitational	Beth Daniel
	Lady Paladin Invitational	Betsy King
	Women's Southern Intercollegiate	Beth Daniel
1978	Lady Tar Heel Invitational	Beth Daniel
	Golden Hurricane Invitational	Beth Daniel
1979	Lady Paladin Invitational	Sherri Turner
	Lady Buckeye Invitational	Sherri Turner
	Women's Southern Intercollegiate	Sherri Turner
1983	Fall Creek Falls Classic	Cindy Davis
1984	Duke Spring Invitational	Dottie Pepper
	Fall Creek Falls Classic	Sara Ann Timms
1985	Carrier Memphis Invitational	Dottie Pepper
	Duke Spring Invitational	Sara Anne Timms

THE PLAYERS
Leading Lady Paladin Returnees

KATHY HART Sr.
Miami Beach, FL

Played very well in two of toughest tourneys last year . . . was 6th in Betsy Rawls and tied for 4th in Women's Southern Intercollegiate . . . 1984 New York women's amateur champ . . . maintains poise under pressure well . . . was 5th in Lady Paladin and at Memphis . . . had a round of 72 at Rawls . . . graduate of Hamburg High.

KRISTIN LOFYE Soph.
Venice, FL

Very talented golfer with great potential . . . one of longest players in college ranks . . . working very hard to improve short game . . . hits a lot of greens . . . was 15th at Alabama Seascape last year and 17th in Lady Paladin . . . 1982 champion at World Series of Junior Golf . . . Captained her Venice High team

DOTTIE PEPPER Jr.
Saratoga Springs, FL . . . NY
Could be poised for great season . . . nominated for Broderick Award as outstanding collegiate golfer in nation . . . brilliant short game . . . tremendous competitor . . . was low amateur in '84 . . . 2nd in NCAA nationals in '85 . . . won Carrier-Memphis and tied with Sara Anne Timms for 1st at Duke, losing playoff . . . sports management major . . . '81 New York state amateur champ and played on PGA Junior International Cup team

KELLIE STENZEL Jr.
Geneva, NY
Number five player a year ago . . . has worked incredibly hard to improve . . . even-par round in NCAA nationals . . . made semis of tough Western Amateur during the summer . . . also lettered in volleyball at Geneva High . . . Business administration major . . . two Top 20 finishes in tourneys last year

MARGARET WILL Jr.
Whiteville, NC

Hits ball well for her size . . . great golf swing . . . looking to improve putting . . . was hampered by back injury during freshman year . . . had a 73 in Lady Seminole for her low round of 1984-85 . . . should be coming into her own . . . won Carolinas PGA Junior Girl title in '82 and was Carolina Junior Girl Golfer of Year that spring

TOP NEWCOMER

DEBBIE MOSS Jr.
Jupiter, FL
Transferred to Furman from Florida State . . . very consistent player . . . hits lots of fairways and keeps ball in play . . . should make major contribution to program . . . had two 6th-place finishes in tourneys while at FSU as freshman

---

FURMAN UNIVERSITY GOLF COURSE

Furman is fortunate to have located on its campus one of the finest university golf courses in the nation.

The 18-hole course measures 6,800 yards for men and 5,800 yards from the women's tees. The par-72 layout makes up 170 acres on the 743-acre campus. Designed by Richard K. Webel, the course was completed in 1959. There are three holes where water comes into play and some 33 bunkers.

The course is the site for numerous tournaments, including the South Carolina state high school championships, the Furman Intercollegiate men's tournament and the Lady Paladin Invitational, which attracts top women's teams.

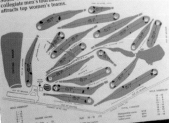

LADY PALADINS IN THE PROS

Beth Daniel
1980 & 1981 LPGA Player of the Year

Sherri Turner

Cindy Ferro
Melissa Whitmire

Beth Solomon   Betsy King 1984 LPGA Player of the Year

1985 NCAA TOURNAMENT FOURTH PLACE FINISHERS

Furman University's women's golf team capped off a highly successful 1984-85 season by finishing fourth in the NCAA tournament after winning three tournament titles during the year. Pictured are, from left, first row—Sara Couture, Kathy Hart, Michelle Carrier; back row, from left—Diane Kohmescher, Karen Charland, Dottie Pepper, Margaret Will, Kellie Stenzel and head coach Mic Potter.

His advice: First, be sure to keep your eye on the ball until it has been struck. Seems simple, but it is human to want to quickly see a result. I sometimes found it helpful in practice to listen to the ball go in, rather than be tempted to sneak that early look. Along these very same lines, I got a wonderful tip from my now colleague at CBS Sports, Ian Baker-Finch, just prior to winning my last LPGA Tour title, the 2000 Arch Wireless Tour Championship. Ian simply told me to not focus on the entire ball but on one dimple, bringing the focus in even tighter and more specific.

Second, Mr. Pulver wanted me to experiment with feeling the putter more in my right hand as a right-hand dominant player. I still have better feel in my right hand despite the activities he suggested to balance out my right and left hands. What comes naturally will be most reliable, most instinctive when the pressure is greatest.

And finally, to let go just a bit. He felt I was trying so hard, and tension was winning the battle. It's such a difficult thing for so many to do, myself included, but so important. How often have we heard athletes say when asked why they had success, "Well, I just tried to have some fun out there today." It takes discipline to have fun, to find that magical ratio between grind and giggle that not only results in wins but an enjoyably balanced life.

I responded to Mr. Pulver, thanking him for his continued advice, not knowing it would be his last from a typewriter. Looking back now, it's remarkable how clean his typing was that day, given the pain it must have caused.

19 OCTOBER 1985

DEAR MR. PULVER,

THANKS SO MUCH FOR WRITING BACK SO QUICKLY AND FOR SENDING THE CRENSHAW ARTICLE ON PUTTING. I ENJOYED BOTH YOUR LETTER AND THE ARTICLE AND AM HAVING MUCH MORE SUCCESS ON THE GREENS THAN WHEN I LAST WROTE. I HAVE DEFINITELY PUT IN MY FAIR SHARE OF HOURS WITH MY SHORT GAME IN THE PAST WEEK, BUT HAVE REALLY ENJOYED IT BECAUSE I'M BEGINNING TO SEE RESULTS. I HAVE CONCENTRATED ON WATCHING THE BALL LEAVE BEFORE MOVING MY HEAD, APPROACHING EACH PUTT WITH A POSITIVE ATTITUDE, AND REPEATING MY BEST STROKES AS MANY TIMES AS I CAN. IT JUST TAKES TIME, I GUESS. WE ARE LEAVING THURSDAY FOR THE TOURNAMENT AT DESTIN, FLA. — FANTASTIC GOLF COURSE!

CLASSES ARE GOING A LITTLE BETTER. WE'RE AT "MIDTERM" THIS COMING WEEK --- IT CERTAINLY IS GOING FAST. IT SEEMS AS THOUGH I JUST GOT HERE. THE WEATHER HAS BEEN ABSOLUTELY INCREDIBLE. WE REALLY NEED RAIN, BUT EACH DAY HAS BEEN 80-85° WITH LOTS OF SUN AND VERY LOW HUMIDITY. I DON'T REMEMBER IT BEING THIS WARM SO LATE IN THE YEAR AT ANY TIME DURING MY OTHER YEARS HERE. I'M NOT COMPLAINING, THOUGH; IT'S GREAT GOLF WEATHER!

EVERYONE AT HOME IS DOING WELL. DAD IS DOING LESS TRAVELLING NOW, MOM IS WORKING AT THE ALPINE SHOP AGAIN AS WELL AS TAKING A CLASS DURING THE EVENINGS AT THE HIGH SCHOOL. JACKIE WILL BE GETTING THE BRACES OFF HER TEETH IN 2 WEEKS -- SHE CAN'T WAIT TO BE RID OF THEM. HOW IS YOUR FAMILY DOING? HOW ARE YOU FEELING? ARE YOU KEEPING YOURSELF BUSY? I'M PLANNING ON

SPENDING MY FALL BREAK FROM OCT. 30 - NOV. 3 A
ATLANTA CC WORKING ON MY GAME. IT'S AN INC
IBLE FACILITY. I'M ALSO GOING TO TRY TO GET I
TOUCH WITH JEAN. SHE WASN'T AT HOME THERE WHE
I WAS LAST THERE.

WELL, I GUESS I'D BETTER GET GOING. I'VE GOT
A LITTLE MORE WORK TO DO BEFORE I CAN GO TO SLEE
TAKE CARE OF YOURSELF AND I LOOK FORWARD TO HEAR-
ING FROM YOU.

MISS YOU ALOT.

FONDLY,
Dottie

"I have concentrated on watching the ball leave before moving my head, approaching each putt with a positive attitude and repeating my best strokes as many times as I can. It just takes time, I guess." — Dottie Pepper

With Mr. Pulver's health continuing to slip, I searched out help from other professionals but nothing clicked — too much theory, too many mechanical thoughts, not enough feel. In fact, by Thanksgiving and an upcoming trip to represent the United States in the collegiate matches versus Japan, I was in such a funk that I called Dad and he, along with my sister, drove from home to Greenville the day after Thanksgiving. They found me on the back of the range at Furman — in pouring rain and 45-degree temperatures — with my book of letters from Mr. Pulver, trying to put the pieces back together. Three dawn-to-dusk days and some pretty raw hands later, we had it back on track. Back to basics again. Square alignment, low and slow take away, good extension, full shoulder turn, and taking my time in the transition from the top, beginning the downswing with my left side. How many times did I have to learn that lesson? Apparently, many.

I would return home from a successful trip to Japan and be able to spend time with Mr. Pulver over the Christmas break. He gave me Bobby Jones' *Golf is my Game* to re-read as I headed back to school for the winter term. Of all the books he had, this is the one most underlined. If re-reading the earlier Sarazen was gold, this Jones do-over was platinum. Pages 39-80 are the fundamentals of the game espoused by Jones, passed on with Mr. Pulver's own polish — the parts he knew I would continually need to reacquaint myself with.

On Jan. 5, 1986, I wrote Mr. Pulver yet again. It was my usual mix of school and golf updates, and sharing my gratitude for all the things he had taught me. Little did I know it would be my last letter to him.

Eleven days after I mailed the letter, I received a call from home. Mr. Pulver had passed at the age of 87.

Thankfully, he died at home.

5 JAN 1986

DEAR MR. PULVER,

I'VE GOT A FEW MINUTES BEFORE I RETIRE FOR THE EVENING, BUT WANTED TO DROP A FEW LINES TO YOU BEFORE THAT.

I GOT BACK TO SCHOOL YESTERDAY AND REGISTERED FOR MY CLASSES TODAY. I WILL BE TAKING MACROECONOMICS, SPANISH LITERATURE, AND BADMINTON THIS TERM.

I GOT A CHANCE TO PLAY 9 HOLES AND PRACTICE THIS MORNING. IT WAS A PERFECT DAY — FAIRLY WARM FOR JANUARY AND VERY SUNNY. I STARTED READING THE BOBBY JONES BOOK, GOLF IS MY GAME, AGAIN YESTERDAY AND AM TOTALLY AMAZED BY THAT BOOK EACH TIME I OPEN IT. I HOPE THAT BY READING IT MY CONCENTRATION, CONFIDENCE, AND COURSE MANAGEMENT WILL IMPROVE. ALL THREE HAVE BEEN LACKING A GREAT DEAL LATELY. I'VE GONE BACK TO THE BASICS THAT YOU STRESSED AND TAUGHT ME SO THOROUGHLY; I SEE IT TO BE MY ONLY WAY TO REACH MY POTENTIAL. I OWE YOU SO MUCH FOR INSTILLING ME WITH THE DESIRE TO BE THE BEST PLAYER I CAN -- AND BY FUNDAMENTALS AND SIMPLICITY INSTEAD OF MECHANICALNESS, WORRYING AND GIMICKRY.

WELL — I SUPPOSE IT IS TIME FOR ME TO GET SOME SLEEP.

▼▼ DOSHISHA

- 2 -

TOMORROW PROMISES TO BE A LONG DAY — ESPEC-IALLY WITH AN 8:00 AM CLASS!

I HOPE YOU'RE FEELING BETTER AND THAT YOUR SPIRITS ARE HIGH! YOU ARE FOREVER IN MY THOUGHTS AND PRAYERS.

WITH MUCH THANKS, ADMIRATION, AND LOVE,
Pattie

Obituaries

George J. Pulver Sr., Was Golf Professional

SARATOGA SPRINGS — George Joseph Pulver Sr., a golf professional at McGregor Links and Saratoga Golf and Polo Club, died yesterday morning at his residence after a long illness. He was 87.

* * *

Mr. Pulver was a founding member of the Northeastern New York section of the Professional Golfers Association and the Northeastern Golf Course Superintendents Association.

The Saratoga Springs native designed the first Saratoga Spa course as a layout for cardiac patients and the course at Brookhaven Golf Club in Corinth.

This past year, he was a golf consultant at Brookhaven Golf Club and at International Paper Company's Course in Hamilton Lake.

He coached local golfer Dottie Pepper, presently ranked fifth in the nation and a student at Furman University in Greenville, S.C.

A graduate of Saratoga Springs High School and Albany Business College, he was a cub reporter at the Saratogian in 1922 and became an assistant at the Lake Placid Club Golf Course in 1923. The following year, be began his longtime affiliation with McGregor Links.

He was a golf professional at the Bahamas Golf Club in Nassau, the Lake Placid Golf Club, and the Florida Golf Club in Tarpon Springs.

Mr. Pulver was associated with the local section of the PGA for 58 years, was one of the oldest members in the United States at the time of his death, and was granted a life membership. He also was a 50-year member of the Northeastern Golf Course Superintendents Association and a longtime member of the Saratoga chapters of the Elks and Veterans of Foreign Wars.

He was attached to the British Army during World War I and was wounded in Ypres, France.

He resided at 136 East Ave.

His wife, Martha Walsh Pulver, died in 1981.

Survivors include a son, George J. Pulver Jr. of Catskill; two daughters, Jean Pulver Hague of Atlanta, Ga., and Madelyn Pulver Jennings of Washington, D.C.; and six grandchildren.

A mass of Christian burial will be celebrated at 9:30 a.m. tomorrow at St. Clement's Church. Calling hours are from 2 to 4 and 7 to 9 p.m. today at the William J. Burke and Sons Funeral Home, 628 N. Broadway.

The call came to my dorm room mid-evening. My roommate, Elizabeth, was studying somewhere else on campus, and I was alone. I certainly wasn't surprised by the news, but its finality was still a shock. Mr. Pulver was gone.

I couldn't just sit in the room by myself, so I left a note for Elizabeth that Mr. Pulver had died. She knew how much he meant to me. I didn't want her to worry about me, but I needed fresh air and space. I walked the campus for a while and ultimately ended up having a good cry in the piano parlor room beneath the women's dorms, returning back to our room in the early morning hours.

Unable to afford the last-minute airplane ticket home for his funeral, I turned to my typewriter as a tribute to Mr. Pulver, writing a column for his former newspaper, the *Saratogian*. It's the same paper where Mr. Pulver, as a cub reporter, was told by the owner to read and report on a new book by Seymour Dunn — because he was the only one who understood the game of golf.

That tribute piece ran Wednesday, January 29th, 1986.

I called him my best friend. He was.

Area golfer pays homage to Pulver

The recent death of my best friend and mentor, George Pulver, has prompted me to write this letter. He was truly a one-of-a-kind person — full of love and respect for his fellow man and profession; one who always gave much more than he received and who deeply touched the lives of nearly every person he came into contact with.

I have known Mr. Pulver since I was 7 years old, but for the last five years, we shared a very special relationship both on and off the golf course. Somehow, I never could find "just the right words" to tell him what he meant to me personally and professionally. I hope that you can find a small section of the newspaper to print the following dedication. Maybe this time I have found a way to say thank you to Mr. Pulver.

Somehow I never managed to find the right words to tell you how much I love and admire you, how much you will always mean to me.

Ever since I was 10, sneaking onto the driving range when you were there in hopes that you would spare me a few minutes and some guiding words, until just a month ago, when your last words to me were: "Dottie, your time will come; just always watch the club strike the ball," I knew there was a special something between us.

For five years, you carefully and slowly gave me the building blocks of my career. You stood in cold winds, rain and hot sun, watching me hit golf ball after golf ball, never saying much, but constantly analyzing and only making brief comments as you saw proper. You listened to me cry, complain and exault in victory, knowing all the time that things were progressing just the way you wanted them to. Despite all of it, you never once would take an ounce of credit.

You made me appreciate the game, and above all, you instilled within me, as you called it, "matchless, undiminished determination and the will to win." You always said it is not your wins and losses, but rather the manner in which you search for excellence that remains to the very end. Maybe that is something we all need to remember.

Mr. Pulver, thank you for being the greatest teacher ever, and mostly for being my best friend.

Dottie Pepper
Furman University
Greenville, S.C.

TOURNAMENT RECORD

1985 - (Age 19-20)

- T-7 Patty Sheehan/San Jose State Invitational, Fort Ord C.C.

- T-30 Betsy Rawls Invitational, Great Hills C.C.

- 4th place, Lady Paladin Invitational, Furman University Golf Course

- 3rd place, Lady Gamecock Invitational, Woodlands C.C.

- T-1 (lost in playoff) Duke Spring Invitational, Duke University Golf Course

- T-28 WSIC/University of Georgia, University of Georgia Golf Course

- T-2 NCAA Championship, New Seabury Golf Course

- 3rd place, Eastern Amateur, Prince Georges Country Club

- Winner, Futures Tour/Albany Colonie Open, Town of Colonie Golf Course

- T-1 (won in playoff) Gail Sykes Best Ball Championship, Ballston Spa C.C.

- 3rd place low amateur, U.S. Women's Open, Baltusrol Golf Course

- T-12 in stroke play play qualifying, lost in the 3rd round of match play. U.S. Women's Amateur, Fox Chapel C.C.

- Winner, Capital District Open, McGregor Links C.C.

- T-4 Lady Seminole Invitational, Florida State Golf Course

- T-15 Lady Buckeye Invitational, Ohio State University Scarlet Course

- T-40 Memphis State Invitational, Stonebridge C.C.

- 5th place, Alabama-Seascape Invitational, Seascape Resort

- T-23 Pat Bradley/FIU Invitational, Key Biscayne Golf Course

Chapter 7

In the years following Mr. Pulver's death, I worked with some outstanding teachers, including Jack Conger, Mic Potter, Ted Ossoff, Kandi Comer, and Craig Harmon. I even leaned on Dad, because he knew my swing and tendencies from the very beginning. I benefitted enormously from each, taking from them, as Mr. Pulver always suggested, the things that worked best for me.

George Pulver, Sr., outside his home. Photo courtesy of the Pulver family

Among the highlights from Jack came the belief that every putt is a straight putt; you're just changing where you start that putt. What a simple and liberating thought that is!

Mic was the best at passing along drills that made success during practice more easily translate to success in competition—reinforcing the mindset that if I could complete these drills in practice, where the first shot is as important as the last, I could do the same when a number needs to be put on the scorecard. Mic also said something after my first round as a college freshman at Furman that stuck like Super Glue. He simply said, "Great job." I had never looked at playing golf as a job but he was right — it was my job and a fun one at that.

Ted was a pure fundamentalist with a keen eye for the creativity needed to score with the short game. He caddied for me in my first LPGA Tour win, and it never mattered to him how well or how poorly I hit it. We were just going to find a way to get the ball in the hole faster than anyone else. When I would get worked up about a run of lousy ball-striking he'd say, "It doesn't take much to get a Rolls Royce running right again."

Kandi Comer and Dottie at the 1985 Women's Amateur.
Photo courtesy of Dot Gunnells

Kandi Comer is another fundamentalist who has a special gift for blending old-school thoughts with today's technology. She was my closest friend through college golf and a Curtis Cup teammate; no secrets among us! My body was starting to break down a bit when we worked together, so, regretfully, we never experienced the joy of winning together. I also learned how tough it can be to work with a close pal but also have the gift of a friend for life — and her two kids, too!

Craig had the best way of describing a swing, putting a very vivid picture in your mind. It took mechanics out and replaced it with a clear visualization and feel. For example, "try to launch a ball under the lowest rung on a fence." That was low, trapping extension at its simplest. One of the things Craig and I worked on from the start was keeping my left heel much more on the ground during the backswing, something Mr. Pulver had made note of on a 1984 Polaroid. Guess I'm a little hard headed!

Craig — as well as brothers Butch and Billy — also teach with great humor. The treasure trove of Harmon family golf stories is invariably opened during lessons and one cannot help but learn from them. The stories were a common denominator with Mr. Pulver's teaching and reading assignments, something that really clicked with me.

All three of Mr. and Mrs. Pulver's children were wholeheartedly supportive of me and the relationship I had with their

Craig Harmon continually worked with Dottie to keep her left heel closer to the ground – a problem Mr. Pulver pointed out in this 1984 Polaroid

dad and remained in close contact after his passing. They also gifted me a portion of Mr. Pulver's golf library. Madelyn and I even played in a pro-am at the LPGA Championship where she holed out for eagle at the last hole to win the tournament! After moving home in 2009, I would make my way to Catskill occasionally to visit George, Jr., and his wife, Shelly. Much of George, Sr.'s memorabilia was kept in George, Jr.'s home office overlooking the Hudson River, and what wonderful memories it brought back.

The Honorable George J. Pulver, Jr., passed in the summer of 2015 at age 71 but carried on his dad's letter-writing legacy. Among the letters he copied me on was this one to Jim Moriarty of *Golf Digest* in 1992 after the magazine had run a lengthy piece on me. I had never thought of the relationship with Mr. Pulver as one similar to Cus D'Amato and Mike Tyson or Mr. Miaghi and the Karate Kid, but he was absolutely correct. It was, indeed, a unique relationship between mentor and student. It began at such a sad time with Martha's passing but such purpose and joy came from the next five years together.

PULVER & STIEFEL

COUNSELORS AT LAW

331 MAIN STREET

CATSKILL, NEW YORK

12414

518-943-4330

GEORGE J. PULVER, JR.
EDWARD P. STIEFEL
JOHN W. WINANS

H. MILTON CHADDERDON
COUNSEL
FAX 518-943-2123

October 22, 1992

Mr. Jim Moriarty
c/o Golf Digest
5520 Park Avenue
P.O. Box 395
Trumbell, Connecticut 06611-0395

Dear Mr. Moriarty:

Your instincts, insights, and intuitions set forth in "Game Face" in the November, 1992 issue of <u>Golf Digest</u> borders on genius.

Words are never weaker tools that when one attempts to use them to describe relationships. It's a human limitation of our language. Yet, you most adeptly captured the relationship between Dottie and my father in your writing. Whether it be a Cus D'Amato/Mike Tyson or Mr. Miaghi/Karate Kid, there is a unique, warm, and special relationship that develops between the mentor and the student. The mass appeal is tremendous. Bravo to you for capturing and memorializing it!

In closing, may I say that most children lionize their parents. I truly believe that my father was as knowledgeable as anybody in regard to the game of golf. The history of golf, golf course architecture, clubmaking, teaching, and greenskeeping were a few of the arrows in his professional quiver. Yet, as many focused individuals, he was notoriously poor at self-promotion. They believe their vast talents must be obvious to all the world or they're above it all. I hope your article is the start of a lifetime of positive publicity to a person near and dear to the Pulver Family, namely, Dottie. I hope Dottie becomes more acutely aware of "spin" and "image." She is maturing nicely, but she has not reached the greatest of seasons. Please keep watch.

Very truly yours,

George J. Pulver, Jr.

GJP/ld
cc:
Dottie Mochrie

George, Jr., was also correct in his assessment of his father's golf knowledge. It literally spanned the entirety of the game. There were many arrows in his professional quiver, and he was very happy to live a quiet and understated life, never seeking public affirmation.

Mr. Pulver was inducted into the Northeastern New York PGA Hall of Fame in October 1995. I was so honored that Jean, Madelyn, and George asked me to join them in accepting the award on his behalf. That night, they gave me the first club in my collection of hickory-shafted clubs made by their dad.

From left, Jean, George, Jr., Dottie and Madelyn. Photo courtesy of NENY PGA

At the ceremony, George, Jr., said of the time and work Mr. Pulver and I did together, "Their relationship was the richest and warmest one you could imagine. He loved her and he marveled with her. Their relationship will never change and will never be superseded or bettered." He was right.

A later letter from George, Jr., landed in my mailbox after I sent him a copy of Jimmy Roberts' *Breaking the Slump*. Jimmy and I were colleagues at NBC Sports at the time and he had so kindly asked me to be a part of his book after hearing my many stories about Mr. Pulver.

GREENE COUNTY COURTHOUSE
80 Woodland Avenue
CATSKILL, NY 12414

HON. GEORGE J. PULVER, JR.
COUNTY JUDGE

Telephone (518) 943-2171
Facsimile (518) 943-3014

May 21, 2009

Dear Dottie:

Thank you so much for <u>Breaking The Slump</u> by Jimmy Roberts.

In Chapter 15, you and Jimmy Roberts have, as to the game of golf, painted a perfect picture of my father, the artisan, the philosopher, and the shaman.

As you must know, my dad loved you dearly. You were to him one of his children. I always kidded him till the end that you were the champion that he wanted me to be.

He would always say "She will be a great champion, as sure as morn follows evening". (People can't believe he actually spoke in those terms.)

Like father, like son, my best to your mom and dad.

See you down the road.

Love,

P.S. I have a box of material of which you are the subject matter. I will get it to you one of these days.

Program

Remembering Martha and George Pulver

PLACE First Tee

DATE Monday, August 13, 2001

TIME 10:30 AM - Refreshments
11:00 AM - Dedication

REMARKS Mike Shpur
Hon. William L. Ford
Al Mottau
Josephine (Jo) Taylor
Bert Edwards
Dottie Pepper
The Pulver Children

Please RSVP to (518) 584-6270
before August 1st.

The Pulver children commissioned a stone bench to be placed on the first tee at McGregor Links in their parents' honor and memory in 2001. "It was a tribute to two people who not only made golf a better place but the people around them better every day they were with us," said Dottie. Here is the program produced for the dedication and the bench itself.

George, Jr., again found the right words to further describe his dad as he was, indeed, an artisan, philosopher and shaman. His dad also loved to serve others. But it was the way George, Jr., articulated his dad's feelings for me that still makes me reach for the tissues. In many ways I did become his fourth child. And as many children do, I look back and wish I could have been more like him in doing things with his kind-but-firm manner. What I am so grateful for is the relationship I still have with his children, and now even their children.

(For more from George, Jr., please see the addendum on Page 188.)

Yes, Mr. Pulver would be embarrassed to have this much attention paid to him but worse would be these letters staying in my office, in their aging three-ring binder and not being shared with others.

As Mr. Pulver would often sign off, I will do the same:

Hang in there. No reply is expected.

Addendum

Just days before this book was to go to the printer, a magical thing happened. I was on my way across town to the chiropractor, then to do a voiceover for the video trailer about the book. But I made my usual stop first to check our post-office box.

In our box was a thick, legal sized envelope from Madelyn, George, Sr.'s daughter. This wasn't so unusual. She'd been going through old files, and that's exactly what her note said: "Going through some old files. XO, M."

COUNSELORS AT LAW
331 MAIN STREET
CATSKILL, NEW YORK
12414

518-943-4330

H. MILTON CHADDERDON
COUNSEL

GEORGE J PULVER, JR
EDWARD P. STIEFEL
JOHN W WINANS

March 31, 1986

Dottie Pepper
P.O. Box 27934
Furman University
Greenville, South Carolina 29613

Dear Dottie:

I intended to write you shortly after my father's passing but my involvement in a multi-week trial prevented such communication.

It seems that at each of our past meetings I was either trying to uplift my failing father in his last days, or rushing and pressing to accomplish something that, at the time, seemed so very important. In any event, I've never had an adequate opportunity to do any more than exchange light pleasantries; so please indulge me while I now take this time to say a little more.

As my mind goes back four years to my mother's demise, I see a terribly pained shell of a man; confused, beside himself with grief.... a man who enjoyed a symbiotic relationship with a woman.... his wife.... who had bore him three children, but the progeny were out in the world, carrying on their own lives in, seemingly to him, "distant places". Isolation, individualism, intellectualism were just a few sides to this many-faceted, but very warm person.... but these three facets seemed exaggerated without the stable and leveling influence of his wife and friend, Martha. Thus, he was adrift and askew.

The three children, who loved him dearly, were gravely concerned. What was the proper "medicine"?

Then, like a script from a 1930's movie, indeed a gift from the gods themselves, a sensitive, and uncommonly bright sixteen year old requests they form a twosome. The rest is history. He claimed your successes were and will be inevitable. "Indeed", he said, "she is and will be a champion, surely as morn follows evening". Moreover, in the quiet moments of the closing days, I would detect his immense love, admiration and affection of you and what you brought to the twilight of his career.

But most of all, his pride swelled, believing that he had subliminally imparted to you an intangible and immeasurable force that will, in the face of adversity, cause victory. As Dan Fogelberg in the song "Leader of the Band" metaphorically states, "your blood runs through my instrument, your song is in my soul" in memory of his father; so too, GJP's blood runs through the clubs that are your instruments and so too, his song is in your soul. What was his song?

As his pupils look back upon him, and you as surely as I, are one of the many pupils who sat at his feet and listened to his wisdom; the philosophy of his profession and life were clear. It was a bit of Walter Hagen, a trace of Socrates, a whisper of Ben Hogan and a hint of Buddha.

Basically, he believed that if you undertake to do something, do it to the very best of your ability. You may not be the best on a given day, but you must strive to be the very best that you yourself can be. Moreover, he believed you take one day at a time, but most of all, it isn't where you've been, it's where you're going. Don't look back! "George, your victories may seem too great or insignificant, your losses may appear too minimal or too important....You accomplish, be a doer, let the non-doers be your historians. Dottie, when at your last meeting Dad said, "Keep your eye on the ball", I believe he meant the ball of life. Now, today, and tomorrow were more important than yesterday to him. He had a great zest for life, present and future.

In another vein, as I prepared for a trial a few years ago, the hours and details of the undertaking had virtually sacked me. As I explained the matter to my father, his analysis caused me to eventually be victorious. Remember, "take one hole at a time"....better yet, take a "shot at a time"...."A masterpiece in art is made up of a minimal amount of well executed brush strokes by a master concentrating on each stroke alone, and then in the fullness of time, creating an extraordinary work of art". I suspect he saw little difference between brush strokes on a canvas and golf strokes on a course. I suspect he saw little difference between each stroke on a canvas and each day of his life. Yet, despite the discipline of the "Master" that he esposed, he was fond of quoting Walter Hagen's famous quote.... "Don't hurry, don't worry, and don't forget to smell the flowers along the way". He believed that life's greatest prospect lies before you. i share his belief.

In closing, may I wish you every success academically and athletically for the year of 1986. Perhaps we can play a round this summer. Please send my regards to your mother and father.

Sincerely,

George J. Pulver, Jr.

What is beyond odd, however, was that the envelope contained a copy of a typewritten letter addressed to me while I was at Furman University. It was from George, Jr., written just weeks after his father's death.

I had never seen this letter until that afternoon! Either George, Jr., never mailed the original, or it was lost in the mail. Obviously, he had sent a copy to Madelyn. I sat in the car, reading it … teary-eyed. It explains perfectly the relationship between me and Mr. Pulver. It is everything we accomplished, summed up in two pages.

Like so much regarding Mr. Pulver, this was meant to be. And so I've shared it here.

— Dottie

Acknowledgements

There are so many to thank when one takes on a project such as this, but my first thank you goes to the One who gave me such peace and guidance on this journey. When He puts you on a road, it's time to take your hands off the wheel and give up the control you too often crave.

Telling Mr. Pulver's story, what he meant to me, and the lessons that are still relevant today would not have been possible without the unconditional and enthusiastic support of the entire Pulver family. Jean, Madelyn, Shelly (George, Jr.'s widow), and even the grandchildren — Ann, Liz and John — all dug through their homes looking for photos and documents. Their response to the idea of the book was overwhelming, and their trust in me to tell their dad's story is treasured.

Imagine writing a book with an editor you've never met and only knew because of a distant connection of Mr. Pulver's daughter, Madelyn. Now imagine him embracing not only the project but the spirit of it. He "got it" instantly. Thank you, Doug Weaver, for not only agreeing to personally take on this book but pushing me to, as you said, "turn yourself inside out" for the reader. There was no ghostwriter involved. Just my writing, and Doug understanding the relationship between me and Mr. Pulver, and how best to get that on paper.

And now imagine that your designer and his team never met your editor, except through the magic of Zoom! Martin Miller, you have been a trusted friend for years but your guidance on this entire journey has been straight from your heart. I trusted you with my relationship with Mr. Pulver, and you and Doug have worked with such ease and symmetry. Thank you, Tim Cottrill, for working with Martin so closely on the design. Thank you, too, Ruth Campbell for your fine copy editing and proofreading.

Early on, it became apparent that we needed a timeline to do Mr. Pulver's life justice. M.K. Rotenberry, you didn't hesitate when I asked you to take on this detailed research, connecting with not only the Pulver family members for their history but also pulling together others in the golf world such as PGA of America Historian Emeritus Bob Denney, Pete Trenham, and the NENY PGA's Doug Evans. Because Mr. Pulver didn't like to talk about himself or his accomplishments, you had quite a task on your hands. As we say when you are at my side at CBS, "You killed it." Thank you, Critter.

I pestered Mom and Dad for specifics of Dad's time in baseball, his dad's death, the turkey farm and Duffer's Den — all important pieces of the early story of how we all came to know Mr. Pulver and his family. You sacrificed so much to give me the opportunities I had. Thank you for digging through so many boxes of photos and sharing memories I know weren't always great ones. He had a bigger plan there, too.

The support of Augusta National Golf Club, the PGA of America (especially Kathy Jorden and Corinne Hanna), Andrew Hickey and his team at the New York State Golf Association, the town of Greenfield, New York, Somerset Hills C.C., and the USGA Museum has been humbling and so appreciated. Thank you, too, to Sandi Higgs from the LPGA who jumped through hoops for us in gathering certain photographs.

Finally, Dr. Barry Johnson: When there were a few potholes in the road, you were there to help show me how to avoid them. You're still a wicked bet on the golf course, but I love ya.

Afterword by Mike Tirico

Why.

It is such a short word that can lead to so many answers as we unlock a question. So why ... amongst thousands of young, talented golfers and hundreds of successful professional golfers ... why has Dottie Pepper lived such an accomplished and impactful life?

Well, now we know why.

In this incredible collection of personal memories, what stands out (other than Dottie's sweet-as-her-swing penmanship) are the principles that formed the friend so many of us admire today. These letters, containing a connective fiber of foundational golf and life lessons, were the seeds from which greatness blossomed.

We all cross many intersections in life, never really knowing when a turn will bring about sharing a road with someone who makes the ride more enjoyable.

I am sure that my days on the ESPN SportsCenter desk in the early 1990s included narrating highlights from a few of Dottie's 17 LPGA wins. But my first time truly getting to know Dottie came in the late '90s while starting a career covering golf at ABC and ESPN.

During LPGA events, my time in the host tower gave me the incredible opportunity to work with Hall of Famer Judy Rankin. So many of the traits we learned about George Pulver, Sr., in this book also define Judy and her one-of-a-kind late husband, Yippy. The Rankins' judgment and words were always enlightening, impactful, and intentional. Their endorsement of Dottie as one of the "all-time good people" was enough for me. They could not have been more accurate.

Following Judy's glass-ceiling-breaking path, Dottie has forged a true landmark career in sports television. It has been inspiring to watch her transition from major champion to one of the most familiar and respected voices covering men's golf. She is one of the rare announcers who has worked all four majors, an accomplishment highlighted by her groundbreaking assignments at the Masters.

Dottie helped make our ESPN golf team one of the most enjoyable ensembles I have been a part of during my now four-decade career. Her insight and expertise have been seen by millions. But what stands out for me is what the viewers never get to see – her behind-the-scenes laughter, friendship, and sacrifice, which helped foster an uncommon esprit de corps within our group.

This window into Dottie's early days has helped me understand how a determined, hard-working teen took the inspiring words of a great teacher and became one of the most engaging figures in the sport. A champion on the course and more importantly a champion for those around her. George's lessons, like the game itself, provided so many parallels for success in life. Now decades later, it is Dottie who is doing the same.

Her work and words continue to bring education and enjoyment to generations of golfers around the world. Dottie always comments how wonderful a work experience she has walking inside the ropes with some of the best in the world. We are all so fortunate to have Dottie taking us on the journey with her.

Mike Tirico has been a broadcaster with NBC Sports since 2016. Prior to NBC, he spent 24 years with ABC and ESPN, anchored SportsCenter, and covered a variety of sports, including golf, college football, tennis, the NBA, NHL, NFL, and World Cup soccer.

INDEX

INDEX

INDEX